THE

greencitymarket

COOKBOOK

THE greencitymarket
COOKBOOK

GREAT RECIPES FROM
CHICAGO'S AWARD-WINNING
FARMERS MARKET

MIDWAY

AN AGATE IMPRINT

CHICAGO

Printed in the United States
All photographs copyright © Chris Cassidy Photography Inc.

Library of Congress Cataloging-in-Publication Data
Green City Market cookbook : great recipes from Chicago's award-winning
farmers market / edited by Green City Market.
    pages cm
 Includes index.
 Summary: "A guide to preparing organic, sustainable, and locally sourced
farm products, with recipes from Chicago's leading chefs, and from farmers,
volunteers, and shoppers of the Green City Market"-- Provided by publisher.

 ISBN-13: 978-1-57284-157-4 (flexibound)
 ISBN-10: 1-57284-157-5 (flexibound)
 ISBN-13: 978-1-57284-736-1 (ebook)
 ISBN-10: 1-57284-736-0 (ebook)

1. Cooking (Natural foods) 2. Local foods--Illinois--Chicago. 3. Green City
Market (Chicago, Ill.) I. Green City Market (Chicago, Ill.)
 TX741.G744 2014
 641.3'02--dc23
                          2013048693

10 9 8 7 6 5 4 3 2 1

Midway Books is an imprint of Agate Publishing. Agate books are available in
bulk at discount prices. For more information, go to agatepublishing.com.

Abby Mandel, my friend and the founder of Green City Market, described her food as "the earthy robust flavors of a simple cuisine." She valued knowing the farmers who grew her ingredients, and she celebrated each season of the Midwest's bounty. Abby fostered the feeling of community around food by gathering people at the table for a home-cooked meal prepared with care and appreciation for the local farm produce she valued. Abby died in 2008, but her principles still guide us.

That is why, when a cookbook was suggested that featured the best recipes from the Green City Market family of customers, chefs, volunteers, vendors, and farmers, I knew it was just what Abby would have wanted. She would be so proud of this important milestone for the Market. This book represents the essence of her values and of the community spirit of Green City Market.

Sarah Stegner
GREEN CITY MARKET FOUNDING MEMBER
AND BOARD CO-CHAIR

Contents

Foreword

By any measure, the numbers are astounding. Thirteen years. More than 60 farmers. Crowds of 10,000 or more. Year-round.

Green City Market statistics become even more astounding when you find out how it all started: as a tiny, nine-vendor market in a hidden alley next to The Chicago Theatre.

At first, the Market almost didn't make it. Yes, it was "different" from other farmers markets; it was the one enthusiastically embraced by chefs and foodies. Yes, it was a market with a laser focus on sustainability. And yes, it was a market that focused on teaching kids and cooks about the richness of our local bounty and how to create delicious preparations with it.

But by 2000, two years after my friend Abby Mandel—the pioneering food writer and Midwest food champion—started Green City, the Market had gained minimal traction. Held only on Wednesdays back then, it had few vendors and only a few more patrons. Worse still, Abby was feeling overwhelmed and dejected. She had half a mind to throw in the towel.

To me, that was a horrifying thought. After opening Frontera Grill in 1987, and after many years living near and cooking from the unique regional markets of Mexico, Green City was the first real hope I'd had that I might be able to source incomparable ingredients from the Midwest and offer our guests a distinctive Chicago experience. As I dreamed of local and sustainable options, it appeared that many of my fellow chefs had embraced the opposite: On their menus, it seemed, the farther an ingredient had traveled, the more prestige it had.

The idea of a twice-a-week market where I could buy the bulk of my produce from local farmers—well, that was still a dream.

But it was a dream worth chasing. So a meeting was called. A group of chefs—Paul Kahan, Sarah Stegner, John Bubula, and I among them—decided that if Abby wanted to step down, we would step up. For a while the idea was intoxicating; meeting after meeting, we found ourselves energized, excited, and ready to continue the great work that Abby had started.

Then reality set in. Taking over the Market was no small project, and we had restaurants to run. None of us really had the time to nurture the Market the way it deserved to be done. We needed to put Green City Market in the hands of a passionate food advocate, someone with endless energy and a deep commitment to its values.

In other words, we were in desperate need of Abby Mandel.

Luckily, our discussions about taking over the Market seemed to invigorate Abby. With tenacity and dogged determination, she moved the Market to Lincoln Park. When she expanded the marketing hours to include Saturdays, it took on a whole new life: people saw it as a place not just to shop, but to hang out, learn, share, and get inspired—which was Abby's goal from the beginning.

Was this cookbook part of Abby's plan? As a cookbook writer herself—and I can attest that she found great satisfaction in sharing beautiful recipes to enrich folks' lives as they gather around tables—she would have loved the idea. But it's not just the recipes that Abby would have appreciated. It's the unique inspiration that issues from each page of this book. Abby was a firebrand when it came to how people thought of Midwest foods, and she found no more convincing an argument than a great recipe or a delicious plate of food. Which is exactly what you'll find here.

Rick Bayless
AUGUST 2013

Introduction

The joy of Green City Market is the marvelous variety of top-quality produce and products that our area farmers bring throughout the seasons.

Each week something new reaches its peak, whether it is the bright green asparagus in the spring, the sugar-sweet corn of summer, the hearty and colorful squash of autumn, or the shiny chestnuts ready for roasting and turning into winter soup.

The Green City Market Cookbook is a labor of love from our entire community of farmers, volunteers, chefs, vendors, and customers, all of whom share the belief that fresh, local, and sustainable products are good for our health, our waistlines, our economy, and ultimately our earth.

Cooking wonderful meals with such fine ingredients can be simple and easy. With this book, our goal is to help you explore, in your home kitchen, the wide range of foods available at Green City Market. When you select Market products, you not only satisfy your family's need for delicious and healthful food, you participate in an economy that helps farmers earn a living as they take care of the land.

Our recipes are gleaned from favorites submitted by our community. All have been tested for accuracy, ease of preparation, use of local seasonal products and, most important, for taste.

We have arranged the recipes by season, designed to feature what is freshest and most abundant from local producers. We invite you to sample, savor, and support Green City Market, which brings you the best our region has to offer 12 months a year.

Meet Green City Market

Green City Market is a bustling sustainable farmers market held year-round in Chicago's Lincoln Park. "Know Your Food. Know Your Farmer" are our watchwords.

From its small beginning to its current incarnation as a beehive of food lovers, with some 60 vendors visited by an average of 10,000 people on busy summer days, the goals have been the same. We provide shoppers with a diverse range of high-quality, local, sustainably raised foods, and a marketplace where farmers and local food producers can sell their products. We also educate people in the value of supporting sustainable foods, and inspire them with ideas on how to prepare them.

All Market farmers and vendors must be certified by an independent agency as good stewards of their land and animals. The Market is a 501(c)(3) organization, which relies on community financial contributions to support educational initiatives, including an organic farm in the Lincoln Park Zoo's Farm-in-the-Zoo, weekly chef demonstrations, and a Club Sprouts program for young Market visitors.

We delight in connecting our Market farmers with the people who cook their food, from novices to professional chefs. And we are proud to bring the best of the Midwest farmlands in Illinois, Indiana, Iowa, Michigan, and Wisconsin to Chicago's tables.

About This Book

The Green City Market Cookbook is the result of a collaboration of representatives of the entire Market community. The committee was a hard-working, dedicated, and always congenial band.

Dana Benigno, former Green City Market Executive Director, originated the project and provided invaluable support at each step of the way.

Meme Hopmayer shared her knowledge and advice based on her broad experience in the culinary field and helped test recipes.

Amelia Levin assembled and coordinated the recipes and other written material, edited the recipe headnotes, and wrote the seasonal introductions.

Karen Levin spearheaded the recipe testing, cooking countless dishes and turning some-times imprecise directions into concise instructions for producing tasty delights.

Janine MacLachlan offered her expert culinary insights and counsel, helped test recipes, and provided insights into the marketing process.

Kathy Paddor set the vision and artistic style for the photography and led its social media and marketing efforts.

Marsha Goldsmith Van edited the manuscript, every last page of it.

We had a delicious time.

Virginia Gerst and Elizabeth Richter
EDITORS

Spring

There's nothing like that sense of excitement and anticipation we feel at the first open-air Green City Market in May. Watching the wave of green from the first harvest of the year, it's clear our farmers' hard work has paid off.

Springtime in the Midwest marks a time of growth and possibility. Some say only wine has *terroir*—that unique combination of geology, geography, and climate that influences taste like nothing else. Yet we know that vegetables and fruits can have the same, as we gorge on woodsy asparagus, glowing red radishes, delicate lettuce, sweet strawberries, rhubarb, peas, and more—the short-lived treasures we look forward to each year.

Recipes

Farmstand Strawberry Jam with Balsamic, Rosemary, and Mint

I was inspired to make this jam from Peter Klein's (Seedling Enterprises) wonderful strawberries. I have used this jam as filling in an updated twist on Linzer cookies, and as a garnish for spring cheese plates with local goat cheese and Potter's rhubarb crackers. The recipe is easily doubled. —**Mary McMahon, chef, Elawa Farm**

2 pounds (about 4 cups) fresh strawberries, hulled and halved

1 cup organic sugar

3 tablespoons balsamic vinegar

1 tablespoon fresh lemon juice

¼ teaspoon salt

1 teaspoon chopped fresh rosemary

1 teaspoon chopped fresh mint leaves

Prep time: 15 minutes

Cook time: 1 hour 5 minutes

Makes 16 servings
(2 tablespoons each)

1. In a large, nonreactive saucepan over high heat, combine the strawberries, sugar, vinegar, lemon juice, and salt and bring to a boil. Reduce the heat to medium–low and simmer, stirring occasionally, for about 1 hour, until the mixture is reduced by half.

2. Dip a spoon in the mixture and examine the back of the spoon. If it is evenly coated, stir in the rosemary and mint. (If not, continue cooking until the mixture passes the spoon test.) Continue simmering for 5 minutes. Remove from the heat and set aside to cool.

3. Transfer the mixture to a 16-ounce jar and cover tightly. Store in the refrigerator; the jam will stay fresh in the refrigerator for up to 2 weeks.

Sugar Snap Pea Soup with Leeks and Bacon

This recipe was born of the need to celebrate spring! Fresh peas are some of my favorite foods at Green City Market. The biggest challenge for me is to stop eating them raw from the container they come in so that I can actually make something with them when I get home. Discipline is rewarded with this hearty, fresh-tasting soup, which I first made to feed a crowd for Soup & Bread (a charitable community meal project) at the Hideout music club. Sweet peas, spicy ginger, and bacon—what more could you want?—**Jennifer Berman, customer**

4 slices bacon
1 tablespoon extra virgin olive oil
2 ribs celery, minced
2 shallots, peeled and thinly sliced
1 leek, white and pale green parts only, thinly sliced
1 tablespoon minced fresh ginger
4–5 cups chicken stock or low-sodium chicken broth
2 (4-inch) sprigs rosemary, divided

⅛ teaspoon salt, plus more to taste
⅛ teaspoon white pepper, plus more to taste
1 cup sugar snap peas, thinly sliced
2 cups shelled fresh peas
¼ cup chopped Italian parsley
¼ cup heavy cream
1 to 2 garlic cloves, minced
¼ cup low-fat Greek yogurt
Pea shoots, for garnish (optional)

Prep time: 30 minutes
Cook time: 20 minutes
Makes about 4 to 6 servings

1. In a large saucepan over medium heat, cook the bacon for 3 to 4 minutes, until browned and crisp. Transfer the bacon to a plate lined with paper towels and set aside.

2. Drain all but 1 tablespoon of the bacon drippings from the saucepan and add the oil, celery, shallots, leek, and ginger. Reduce the heat to medium–low and cook for 2 to 3 minutes, until softened but not browned.

3. Crumble 2 slices of the cooked bacon.

4. Add the crumbled bacon, stock, 1 sprig of the rosemary, and the ⅛ teaspoon each of the salt and white pepper to the saucepan. Continue simmering over medium–low heat for 15 minutes, until the vegetables are very tender.

5. Add the sugar snap peas to the saucepan and cook for 3 minutes, until tender and bright green. Add the fresh peas and cook for 2 to 3 minutes, until the peas are crisp-tender. Remove from the heat and stir in the parsley. Remove and discard the rosemary sprig.

6. Using an immersion (stick) blender or a conventional blender, purée the soup to a smooth texture. For a silkier texture, strain the soup through a chinois or other fine strainer (not necessary if you enjoy a heartier soup).

7. In a small saucepan over medium–high heat, bring the cream, garlic, and remaining sprig of rosemary to a boil. Reduce the heat to low and simmer for 5 minutes, until slightly reduced. Remove from the heat.

8. Strain the garlic cream into a bowl and set aside to cool. Season with additional salt and white pepper to taste. Whisk in the yogurt. Set aside.

9. Crumble the remaining 2 slices of bacon. Ladle the warm pea soup into individual bowls and drizzle with the garlic cream. Garnish each bowl with the pea shoots and crumbled bacon.

Spring Vegetable Soup

The Market was the motivating force behind this lovely spring recipe because it is the perfect place to shop for ingredients that bring seasonality and healthfulness together. I like to serve the light yet hearty soup with toasted country bread from Bennison's Bakery.
—**Sharon Olson, customer**

---

3 cups cold water

2 teaspoons kosher salt, divided, plus more to taste

8 ounces baby carrots, peeled and cut in half

8 ounces asparagus spears, trimmed and cut into 2-inch lengths

4 tablespoons organic unsalted butter, divided

1 cup thickly sliced (¼ inch) leeks, white to pale green parts

3 cloves garlic, minced

½ teaspoon freshly ground black pepper, plus more to taste

1½ cups vegetable broth (preferably organic)

8 ounces pattypan squash or baby yellow squash, halved or cut into 1½-inch chunks

1 cup shelled fresh peas

½ cup chopped mixed fresh herbs (such as chives, tarragon, and parsley)

½ teaspoon grated lemon zest

Shaved hard cheese, such as Brunkow Cheese's Little Darling or similar, for garnish (optional)

Prep time: 25 minutes

Cook time: 20 minutes

Makes 6 servings

1. Place a bowl of ice water next to the sink.

2. In a medium saucepan over medium–high heat, bring the water and 1 teaspoon of the salt to a boil. Add the baby carrots and cook for 3 to 4 minutes, until crisp-tender. Add the asparagus during the last minute of cooking. Drain the vegetables and plunge them into the ice water bath to cool. Set aside.

3. In a large, deep skillet over medium heat, melt 2 tablespoons of the butter. Add the leeks and garlic and sauté for 3 minutes, until softened. Season the mixture with the remaining 1 teaspoon of salt and the black pepper.

4. Add the broth and squash to the skillet and raise the heat to high. Bring the mixture to a simmer and then reduce the heat to medium. Cook for 5 minutes, until the vegetables are crisp-tender.

Continued

5. Add the carrots, asparagus, and peas to the skillet. Continue to simmer for 5 to 6 minutes.

6. Add the herbs and lemon zest to the skillet and stir to combine. Remove the pan from the heat. Add the remaining 2 tablespoons of butter and stir into the mixture until just melted. Remove from the heat. Season with additional salt and black pepper to taste if needed.

7. Transfer the soup to shallow bowls and serve hot, garnished with the shaved cheese.

Cavolo Nero and Strawberry Salad

This simple salad of crunchy kale doused with a tart citrus dressing doesn't seem like much, but it is! A friend and I brought it along on an impromptu picnic. There, someone added the sliced strawberries to our bowl, and presto—a Millennium Park picnic tradition was born. The dressing helps tame the crunchy kale, so chilling it for at least an hour is a must. In fact, the salad may even be made in the morning and chilled all day, since the kale is so sturdy.
—**Marilyn Canna, volunteer**

1 large bunch *cavolo nero* (Italian kale), rinsed and dried
2 tablespoons fresh lemon juice
7–8 tablespoons olive oil
½ teaspoon sugar

½ teaspoon salt
½ teaspoon freshly ground black pepper, plus more to taste
1 pint fresh strawberries, hulled and thickly sliced

Prep time: 20 minutes
Chill time: 1 hour
Makes 6 to 8 servings

1. Remove and discard the thick stems from the kale. Cut the leaves on the bias into ½-inch-thick ribbons and place them in a large serving bowl.

2. In a small bowl, whisk together the lemon juice and oil until they are well blended and an emulsion forms. Whisk in the sugar, salt, and black pepper.

3. Pour half the dressing over the kale and toss until evenly coated. If more dressing is needed, add 1 tablespoon of it at a time. Chill the salad for at least 1 hour, or up to 8 hours. The remaining dressing may be refrigerated up to 5 days.

4. Just before serving, add the strawberries to the kale and toss. Season with additional black pepper, if desired.

Artful Asparagus Salad

This is a simple and flavorful salad I love to make in the spring, when many Green City Market farmers have great-tasting asparagus. I love to shop for seasonal vegetables when cooking at home as well as for the restaurant at The Art Institute of Chicago, which allows me to purchase most of our ingredients from the Market. Our philosophy of "local and seasonal" aligns with the Market's mission perfectly. —**Megan Neubeck, executive chef, Terzo Piano**

FOR THE GREEN GODDESS DRESSING:

2 egg yolks

2 tablespoons red wine vinegar

1 tablespoon Dijon mustard

1 cup sunflower or olive oil

⅓ cup packed chopped fresh chives (½ ounce)

¼ cup packed fresh dill sprigs (¼ ounce)

¼ cup packed fresh tarragon sprigs (¼ ounce)

Salt, to taste

FOR THE SALAD:

1 pound asparagus, tough ends trimmed

3–4 green onions

1–2 tablespoons sunflower or olive oil

Salt, to taste

4 ounces frisée, leaves separated from stem

4 ounces mizuna or mixed spring greens

4 ounces bacon or pancetta, cooked crisp and crumbled

2 hard-boiled eggs, peeled and quartered or sliced

Freshly ground black pepper, to taste

Prep time: 25 minutes

Chill time: 30 minutes

Grilling time: 3 to 4 minutes

Makes 2 main-dish or 4 side-dish servings

TO MAKE THE GREEN GODDESS DRESSING:

1. In a blender or food processor, combine the egg yolks, vinegar, and mustard. With the motor still running, slowly drizzle in the oil in a stream, emulsifying the dressing.

2. Add the chives, dill, and tarragon to the mixture and blend or process until the herbs are minced. Season with the salt. Refrigerate for at least 30 minutes, allowing the flavors to blend.

TO MAKE THE SALAD:

1. Preheat the grill to medium–high (350°F to 400°F).

2. In a medium bowl, coat the asparagus and green onions evenly with the oil.

Continued

3. Place the asparagus and green onions on the grill and cook, turning frequently, about 2 minutes for the onions and 3 to 4 minutes for the asparagus, until crisp-tender. Remove from the grill. Sprinkle lightly with the salt and set aside to cool to room temperature.

4. Once the asparagus and green onions have cooled, slice them on the bias into 1- to 2-inch lengths.

5. In a large serving bowl, combine the frisée, mizuna, bacon, asparagus, and onions. Add ¼ cup of the Green Goddess Dressing and toss well; add more dressing if the salad seems dry. (The remaining dressing can be stored in the refrigerator for up to 3 days.)

6. Arrange the salad on serving plates, top with the hard-boiled eggs, and season with the black pepper.

Note: This recipe uses raw egg. Cases of salmonella poisoning have been traced to raw eggs, although this is rare.

Kohlrabi Mash

Kohlrabi is a vegetable that can be perplexing to chefs and home cooks alike on their first attempt. But after you get to know and understand its basic characteristics and upbringing, it becomes an old friend. You begin to long for it at the end of spring, just before the start of summer, at the point when you've had enough asparagus. Its name comes from the German words for cabbage (kohl) and turnip (rübe): essentially, it's a cabbage–turnip.

Unlike a turnip, kohlrabi grows above ground, much like a cabbage, and it tastes more like a peeled broccoli stem. This recipe is easy to make and can truly show off the vegetable's versatility. Whether simply mashed or puréed into a silky mass, it has a weighty and creamy texture but a light and refreshing taste. —**Benjamin Browning, chef/instructor, Kendall College, School of Culinary Arts**

---

1 large baking potato (about 10 ounces), peeled and cut into ½-inch pieces

2 teaspoons sugar

1½ teaspoons kosher or coarse sea salt, plus more to taste

1 large or 2 medium kohlrabi (about 14 ounces)

2 tablespoons unsalted butter

Freshly ground black pepper, to taste

Prep time: 15 minutes

Cook time: 30 minutes

Standing time: 10 minutes

Makes 4 servings

1. In a medium saucepan over medium heat, place the potato, the sugar, and the 1½ teaspoons salt, and cover twice over with water. Bring to a simmer.

2. Meanwhile, use a sharp knife to trim the stalks from the kohlrabi. Peel ⅛ inch of the skin off of the kohlrabi bulb and cut the flesh into ½-inch pieces.

3. Add the kohlrabi to the saucepan and allow the water to return to a simmer. Simmer for 25 to 30 minutes, until the vegetables are very tender. Remove from the heat, cover, and let stand for 10 minutes.

4. Drain and return the vegetables to the same pan over low heat. Cook for 2 to 3 minutes, until all excess water has evaporated. Remove from the heat. Add the butter and mash to the desired consistency. Season with the salt and black pepper and serve.

Spring Peas with Mint

Every spring we look forward to picking the peas from Sarah's garden. Her daughter even loves to eat them right from the vine. At the restaurant, it can be an intense amount of work to prepare them in volume; we were thus very grateful when we discovered that we could buy them from Mick Klug Farm already shelled! At the restaurant, we spread the pea purée on a plate and spoon the fresh peas that pop in your mouth over the purée. This is delicious with a delicate-flavored fish or chicken breast. —**Sarah Stegner and George Bumbaris, chef/owners, Prairie Grass Café**

1 cup lightly salted water
12 ounces shelled spring peas (about 2½ cups)
¼ cup heavy cream, warmed
4 tablespoons unsalted butter, divided
Salt, to taste

1 small green onion, minced
4–6 leaves fresh mint (spearmint), thinly sliced
Fresh mint sprigs and/or pea shoots, for garnish (optional)

Prep time: 15 minutes

Cook time: 5 minutes

Makes 4 servings

1. In a medium saucepan, bring the salted water to a boil. Add the peas to the saucepan and cook for 45 seconds to 1 minute, until tender. (Do not overcook; taste the peas after 45 seconds. If it is early in the season, they will cook very quickly. They are delicious barely cooked.) Remove from the heat. Drain and set aside 1 cup of the peas.

2. Place the remaining peas into a blender. Add the cream and 2 tablespoons of the butter and blend until smooth. Season with the salt. Set aside.

3. In a small sauté pan over medium–low heat, warm the remaining butter. Add the green onion and cook until tender. Stir in the reserved peas and mint and cook for 2 minutes, until warmed through. Remove from the heat.

4. Spread the warm pea purée on 4 serving plates. Top with the pea and onion mixture. Garnish with the mint sprigs and/or pea shoots, if desired.

Roasted Asparagus Lasagna

For the last decade, or at least for as long as I have been shopping at Green City Market, it has become my spring ritual to make this fabulous lasagna as soon as the first asparagus stalks make their appearance. It is a simpler, quicker version of a recipe from Food & Wine *magazine's pasta cookbook, published in the mid-1990s. Roasting the vegetables intensifies their sweetness, which is an important first step, and Pasta Puttana's egg noodles (conveniently sold in an 8-ounce package) are delicious. You can use green or purple asparagus, or both. Purple asparagus turns green when it is cooked, but it is slightly sweeter.*
—Phillippa Cannon, volunteer

---

2 pounds asparagus, trimmed and cut on the
  bias into ½-inch slices
1 bunch green onions, cut into ½-inch slices
2½ tablespoons olive oil, divided
¾ teaspoon salt, divided
3 tablespoons organic unsalted butter
2 tablespoons all-purpose flour

1½ cups whole milk
10 tablespoons whipping cream, divided
8 fresh flat wide egg noodles, uncooked,
  divided
½ pound fresh mozzarella (plain or smoked),
  thinly sliced
1¼ cups grated Wisconsin Parmesan cheese

Prep time: 50 minutes

Baking time: 42 minutes

Makes 4 to 6 servings

1. Preheat the oven to 450°F.

2. In a large bowl, toss together the asparagus, green onions, 2 tablespoons of the oil, and ¼ teaspoon of the salt.

3. Grease an 8- or 9-inch-square glass baking dish with the remaining oil and set aside.

4. On a large, rimmed baking sheet, spread out the asparagus mixture. Bake for 10 minutes, until the asparagus is crisp-tender. Remove from the oven and reduce the oven temperature to 375°F.

5. Meanwhile, make the béchamel sauce. In a medium saucepan over medium heat, melt the butter and the remaining ½ teaspoon of the salt. Whisk in the flour and sauté for 1 minute.

6. Gradually whisk in the milk. Allow the mixture to come to a simmer. Reduce the heat and simmer, whisking frequently, for 3 to 4 minutes, until the sauce has thickened. Remove from the heat.

7. Spread ¼ cup of the sauce in the bottom of the prepared glass dish. Drizzle 2 tablespoons of the whipping cream over sauce. Layer 2 of the noodles on top, followed by ⅓ cup of the sauce, 1 cup of the asparagus mixture, ⅓ of the mozzarella, ¼ cup of the Parmesan, and 2 tablespoons of the cream. Repeat this layering twice, starting with 2 noodles.

8. Top with the remaining 2 noodles, the remaining sauce, 2 tablespoons of the cream, and the remaining ½ cup of the Parmesan. Cover the dish with foil (if the dish is very full, lightly coat the foil with olive oil to prevent the cheese from sticking).

9. Bake for 20 minutes. Remove the foil and continue to bake for 20 to 25 minutes, until golden brown and bubbly. Remove from the oven. Allow to rest for 5 minutes before serving.

Fresh Pasta with Sugar Snap Peas and Asparagus

This recipe is a great way to highlight the flavor of two favorite spring vegetables. After a long winter of hearty dishes, this one is light but filling. If you do not have a pasta machine, you may hand-cut the pasta into thicker, fettuccini-like strips, or substitute with 3 cups of cooked and drained spaghetti. If making buy hand, roll out the dough thinly before cutting.

—Ted Dobbels, customer

FOR THE PASTA:

1⅓ cups all-purpose flour

1 cup whole-wheat flour

2 large eggs

¼ cup buttermilk

1 teaspoon extra virgin olive oil

FOR THE SAUCE:

3 cups cold water

1 teaspoon salt, plus more to taste

2 cups cut (1-inch pieces) fresh asparagus

1 cup sugar snap peas, halved diagonally

½ cup buttermilk

½ cup chicken stock or broth

1 tablespoon all-purpose flour

½ teaspoon sugar

1 tablespoon extra virgin olive oil or vegetable oil

1 clove garlic, minced

Freshly ground black pepper, to taste

Prep time:
  pasta, 25 minutes
  sauce, 10 minutes

Cook time: 10 minutes

Makes 4 servings

TO MAKE THE PASTA:

1. Combine all the ingredients in a food processor. Pulse until small crumbs form and then turn out the mixture onto a lightly floured surface. Knead the mixture until a smooth dough forms.

2. Wrap the dough in plastic wrap and set aside to rest at room temperature for 30 minutes.

3. Using a pasta machine set to the desired thickness (#3 is preferred), process the dough into sheets. Run the pasta sheets through a cutter to make a spaghetti shape. Separate ½ of the pasta for this recipe; shape the remaining pasta into small nests and freeze for later use.

1. Place a bowl of ice water next to the sink.

2. In a medium saucepan over medium–high heat, bring the water and 1 teaspoon of the salt to a boil. Add the asparagus and sugar snap peas and cook for 2 to 3 minutes, until crisp-tender. Remove from the heat. Drain the vegetables and plunge them into the ice water bath to cool. Set aside.

3. In a large bowl, combine the buttermilk and broth. Whisk in the flour and sugar and set aside.

4. In a large nonstick skillet, warm the oil over medium heat. Add the garlic and sauté for 1 to 2 minutes. Add the buttermilk mixture and simmer until the sauce thickens slightly, 3 to 4 minutes. Add the vegetables and continue to simmer for 3 to 4 minutes, until the vegetables are crisp-tender. Remove from the heat. Season with the salt and black pepper.

5. Meanwhile, bring a large pot of salted water to a boil. Cook the pasta for 1 to 2 minutes, just until al dente. Remove from the heat and drain well, reserving ¼ cup of the pasta cooking water.

6. Toss the vegetable mixture with the pasta, adding the pasta water if necessary. Serve immediately.

Creamy Polenta with Braised Greens and Mushrooms

PICTURED ON PAGE 40

After we started producing cornmeal at Three Sisters Garden, we discovered the magic of a bowl of slightly sweet polenta with a quick mix of whatever we have in the fridge. Short on time, we are always looking for a good way to get an appealing meal on the table as quickly as possible. I particularly like the earthy flavors of mushrooms and greens, so this dish is an easy choice after a day in the field. It makes a wonderfully rich and satisfying dinner paired with grilled chicken or pork, and it can be ready to eat in under an hour. —**Tracey Vowell, farmer, Three Sisters Garden; Green City Market board member**

1 head garlic, unpeeled, separated into cloves

4 cups milk

1 cup fine white cornmeal

½ teaspoon salt, plus more to taste

¼ teaspoon freshly ground black pepper

2 tablespoons unsalted butter

1 pound fresh oyster and/or shiitake mushrooms, washed, tough stems removed, and cut into bite-sized pieces

1 small white onion, chopped

1 fresh hot pepper, such as serrano or habanero, seeded, minced

2 sprigs fresh thyme leaves

1 bunch Swiss chard, kale, or lamb's quarters, washed, stems removed, and coarsely chopped

½–¾ cup vegetable or chicken stock or broth, divided

1 (2-ounce) piece firm grating cheese, such as Brunkow Cheese's Little Darling

Prep time: 30 minutes

Cook time: 25 minutes

Makes 4 servings

1. Preheat the oven to 350°F.

2. In a large, dry skillet, roast the garlic cloves over medium heat, stirring occasionally, for 8 to 10 minutes, until they begin to brown and the garlic feels soft when squeezed. Remove from the heat. Peel and finely chop the cloves. Set aside.

3. In a large saucepan with a tight-fitting lid over high heat, bring the milk just to a simmer. Reduce the heat to medium and slowly pour in the cornmeal, whisking constantly. Whisk in the salt. When the mixture has thickened slightly, remove from the heat, cover the saucepan, and transfer to the oven.

4. Bake for 10 minutes and then whisk. Bake another 10 minutes and whisk again. If the polenta is too thick, stir in additional milk or water. If it is too thin, cover and return to the oven for 5 minutes. After removing the polenta from the oven, stir in the black pepper and keep warm.

5. While the mixture is baking, melt the butter in a large, deep sauté pan over medium-high heat. Add the mushrooms and roasted garlic and sauté for 4 to 5 minutes, until browned. Add the onion, hot pepper, and thyme and sauté for 5 minutes. Add the chard and ½ cup of the broth. Cook, stirring occasionally, for 6 to 8 minutes, until the chard is tender. If the mixture is dry, add the remaining ¼ cup of the broth. Remove from the heat and season with salt to taste.

6. Spoon the warm polenta into 4 shallow bowls and top with the vegetable mixture. Grate some of the cheese over each bowl before serving.

Creamy Polenta with Braised Greens and Mushrooms
Recipe on page 38

Oyster Mushroom and Spring Onion Frittata
Recipe on page 42

Oyster Mushroom and Spring Onion Frittata

PICTURED ON PAGE 41

This is a very simple, easily customized dish. The recipe is special to me because it is the dish that got me over my "mushroom hump." I used to really hate mushrooms, but after talking with the folks at River Valley Ranch, I now enjoy this dish almost daily for breakfast. The people at River Valley have been extremely helpful in suggesting simple and delicious ways to use their mushrooms. This recipe can easily be expanded to make a larger, fancier frittata (see Cooks' Note). —**Tammy Hsu, customer**

2 large eggs

2 tablespoons milk or cream

⅛ teaspoon salt

⅛ teaspoon freshly ground black pepper

1 tablespoon unsalted butter

1 cup sliced or chopped fresh oyster mushrooms

1–2 spring onions, thinly sliced

Prep time: 5 minutes

Cook time: 8 minutes

Makes 1 serving

1. In a small bowl, whisk together the eggs. Add the milk, salt, and black pepper and whisk thoroughly. Set aside.

2. In a small nonstick skillet over medium heat, melt the butter. Add the mushrooms and onions to the skillet and sauté for 3 to 4 minutes, until golden brown. Add the egg mixture to the skillet and stir well until evenly distributed. Cook for 2 to 3 minutes, until set.

3. Flip the frittata over and cook for 1 minute, until the bottom is set. Remove from the heat.

4. Serve immediately.

You can change things up a little ingredient-wise and expand this dish to serve 6. First, preheat the oven to 375°F. In a large bowl, whisk together 8 eggs. Add ¼ cup of milk or cream and whisk to combine. Whisk in ¼ teaspoon each of salt and freshly ground black pepper. Set aside.

In a nonstick 10-inch ovenproof skillet over medium heat, melt 2 tablespoons of butter. Add 2 cups of sliced mushrooms and 2 thinly sliced spring onions. Sauté for 4 to 5 minutes. (If desired, stir 1 cup of cooked diced potatoes into the skillet mixture and sauté until heated through.) Add the egg mixture to the skillet and cook for 3 minutes, until the eggs on the bottom of the skillet have set.

Transfer the skillet to the oven and bake for 18 to 20 minutes, until the center is set. Remove from the oven. If desired, sprinkle ¼ cup of arugula or watercress and ½ cup of crumbled goat cheese over the frittata before serving.

Roast Leg of Lamb in Garlic–Mint Marinade with Pea Shoot Salad

My mother, Helen, roasted a leg of lamb some Sundays for supper following church. She always put so much care and attention into her cooking that she didn't even realize how detailed her effort was. For example, she would squeeze a lemon over the lamb and then make small incisions in the meat and insert slivers of garlic. Under the leg of lamb, she would place small new potatoes, onions, and more garlic for added flavor. Finally, she made a great pan jus with the delicious lamb drippings. Our family is Armenian, so lamb is a major part of our culture, heritage, and life! —**Carrie Nahabedian, chef/owner, Naha and Brindille; Green City Market board member**

FOR THE LAMB:

1 (4–5-lb) whole bone-in leg of lamb

Kosher salt, as needed

Freshly ground black pepper, as needed

1 cup packed fresh mint leaves, chopped

4 cloves garlic, minced

24 medium-sized firm new red potatoes, halved (if the potatoes are small, use more and leave them whole)

¼ cup olive oil, divided

4 sprigs fresh thyme (optional)

1 head garlic, separated into cloves

⅓ cup white or red wine

FOR THE PEA SHOOT SALAD:

2 teaspoons olive oil

1½ teaspoons sherry wine vinegar

3 ounces (about 4 cups) fresh pea shoots

Shaved radishes (optional)

Prep time: 25 minutes

Standing time: 30 minutes

Cook time: 1 hour 20 minutes

Makes 8 servings

TO MAKE THE LAMB:

1. Butterfly the lamb and remove the bone, excess fat, heavy silverskin, and tendons. Sprinkle the inside and outside of the lamb generously with salt and black pepper. Rub the mint and garlic over the inside and outside of the lamb. Roll the lamb up and tie with kitchen string. Let stand at room temperature for 30 minutes.

2. Preheat the oven to 425°F.

Continued

3. In a large, shallow roasting pan, place the potatoes. Add 2 tablespoons of the olive oil and season with salt and black pepper. Toss well. Place the thyme sprigs (if using) over the potatoes. Add the garlic to the pan. Place the lamb over the potatoes and drizzle the remaining 2 tablespoons of oil over lamb. Roast until nicely browned, about 15 minutes.

4. Reduce the oven temperature to 325°F and continue roasting for 1 hour to 1 hour and 20 minutes (depending on the size of the lamb), until the internal temperature of the thickest part of the meat registers 130°F. Remove from the oven.

5. While the lamb is roasting, test the potatoes by piercing them with a fork. When they are tender, transfer them to a bowl and keep warm.

6. Transfer the lamb to a platter, tent with foil, and let rest for 20 minutes before carving.

7. Place the pan full of drippings over 1 or 2 burners on the stovetop. Add the wine and cook over medium–high heat, scraping the drippings from bottom of pan. Add a splash of water, if needed, and bring to a boil. Stir in any juices from the lamb platter. Remove from the heat but keep warm for serving.

TO MAKE THE PEA SHOOT SALAD:

1. In a medium bowl, whisk together the oil and vinegar. Add the pea shoots and radishes (if using) and toss well.

TO SERVE:

1. Carve the lamb into slices and serve with the warm potatoes and pan juices. Garnish with the salad.

Mushroom, Asparagus, and Fontina Cheese Strata

We developed this recipe for one of our brunch cooking classes. With mushrooms from River Valley Ranch, local asparagus, bread from Bennison's Bakery, and, of course, farm-fresh eggs, it's comfort food bursting with fresh spring flavor. —**Shelley Young, CEO/founder, The Chopping Block**

2 tablespoons extra virgin olive oil

1 large red onion, thinly sliced (about 3 cups)

½ pound cremini mushrooms, sliced (about 4 cups)

1 bunch asparagus, trimmed and cut on the bias into 1-inch pieces (about 3 cups)

¼ teaspoon kosher salt

¼ teaspoon freshly ground black pepper

1½ cups shredded Fontina cheese

1 cup grated Wisconsin Parmesan cheese

Unsalted butter, for greasing

1 (15-ounce) French or Italian baguette, cubed (about 8 cups), divided

9 eggs

2¾ cups whole milk

¼ to ½ teaspoon freshly grated nutmeg

Prep time: 25 minutes

Standing time: 30 minutes

Cook time: 50 minutes

Makes 6 to 8 servings

1. Preheat the oven to 350°F.

2. In a large skillet over medium–high heat, warm the oil. Add the onion and cook, stirring occasionally, for 3 minutes, until lightly caramelized. Add the mushrooms and asparagus and continue to cook for 5 minutes, until just softened. Remove from the heat. Season with the salt and black pepper and set aside.

3. In a medium bowl, combine the cheeses. Set aside.

4. Butter a 9-inch-square glass baking dish. Place ⅓ of the bread cubes into the dish and spread them out. Top evenly with ⅓ of the vegetable mixture. Sprinkle with ⅓ of the cheese. Repeat this layering process 2 more times, finishing with the cheese. (Alternatively, you can assemble and bake this in 6 to 8 individual dishes.) Set aside.

5. In a small bowl, whisk together the eggs, milk, and nutmeg. Pour evenly over the strata. Let stand for 30 minutes so the bread will soak up the liquid.

6. Bake, uncovered, for 45 to 50 minutes, until puffed and golden brown. Remove from the oven and let stand for 5 minutes before serving.

Roasted Rosemary Pork Tenderloin

I love that Green City Market stays open all year long, but I especially get excited when the outdoor season begins in the spring. For this recipe, I buy the pork from Jake's Country Meats or Becker Lane Organic Farm and serve it with lovely spring peas. Often, I'll make a strawberry dessert of some kind to celebrate the season even further. —**Betsy Fimoff, customer**

2 tablespoons Dijon mustard
2 large cloves garlic, minced
1 tablespoon dried rosemary leaves, crushed

2 teaspoons freshly ground black pepper
2 (¾-pound) pork tenderloins

Prep time: 5 minutes
Marinating time: 1 to 2 hours
Cook time: 20 minutes
Makes 4 to 6 servings

1. In a small bowl, combine the mustard, garlic, rosemary, and black pepper.

2. Place the pork in a glass baking dish. Spread the mustard mixture evenly over the top and sides of the meat. Refrigerate for 1 to 2 hours.

3. Preheat the oven to 400°F.

4. Roast the pork for 20 minutes, until the internal temperature reaches 145°F. (The meat will be pink in the center.) Remove from the oven.

5. Transfer the pork to a carving board and tent it with foil. Allow it to rest for 5 minutes. Carve into ½-inch-thick slices and serve immediately.

Best Fresh Fruit Cake Ever

I love to go to Green City Market, look around, and decide which glorious fruit I am going to put into a cake when I get home. In the spring, I like to use rhubarb, but at other times of the year I have tried small Italian plums, peaches, and apricots. This is a very versatile recipe that's easy to make. —**Meme Hopmayer, volunteer**

1 cup plus 1 tablespoon granulated sugar, divided
½ cup (4 ounces) unsalted butter, softened, plus more for greasing
2 large eggs
1 cup all-purpose flour

1 teaspoon baking powder
⅛ teaspoon salt
2 cups thinly sliced fresh rhubarb
1 teaspoon fresh lemon juice
½ teaspoon ground cinnamon
Vanilla ice cream, for serving (optional)

Prep time: 15 minutes
Cook time: 1 hour
Cooling time: 1 hour
Makes 8 servings

1. Preheat the oven to 350°F. Grease a 9-inch springform pan and set aside.

2. In the bowl of a stand mixer, cream together the 1 cup of the sugar and the butter on low speed until light and fluffy. Add the eggs and beat until combined.

3. In a medium bowl, combine the flour, baking powder, and salt. As the mixer runs on low speed, add the dry mixture to the butter mixture in thirds. Continue running the mixer until the mixture is well blended.

4. Spread the batter evenly into the prepared pan. Arrange the rhubarb in concentric circles over the cake batter. Sprinkle the lemon juice over the rhubarb.

5. In a small bowl, combine the 1 tablespoon of sugar and the cinnamon. Sprinkle the mixture evenly over the rhubarb.

6. Bake for 55 to 60 minutes, until the center is set. Remove from the oven. Transfer the cake to a wire cooling rack and cool completely. Serve with the ice cream, if desired.

Summer

By mid-July, the Market is in full swing. From tomatoes and stone fruits as sweet as candy to peppers, zucchini, and eggplant rich with the taste of the sun, the farmstands overflow with the bounty for which we've waited so long.

It's a busy time of the year for farmers, who work hard each day to keep pace with the harvest. We, too, strive to keep up, visiting the Market regularly with ambitious plans for making pickles, pestos, salsas, and preserves that we know we'll crave come winter.

Recipes

Eggplant Caponata with Fennel and Oven-Roasted Tomatoes

Each season, I look forward to picking up my weekly CSA box at the Market. Like a mystery basket in a chef's competition, the package comes with many surprises and cooking possibilities. Once, during the summer, the box included extra eggplants, tomatoes, and some fennel, just in time for a dinner party I was hosting. I wanted to create an appetizer that combined all the produce, so I came up with this dish, figuring it would pair well with a recent Potter's Crackers purchase. Roasting the tomatoes brought out their sweet, earthy flavor even more and turned them into an amazing stand-in for the canned version. The pre-meal snack turned out to be an instant hit. —**Amelia Levin, volunteer**

5–6 medium seasonal heirloom red and/or San Marzano tomatoes

2 medium eggplants, unpeeled, cut into ¾-inch cubes

½ teaspoon salt

½ teaspoon freshly ground black pepper

⅓ cup olive oil

2 small-to-medium red bell peppers, seeded and diced

1 medium bulb fennel, coarsely chopped

1 medium onion, diced

6 large cloves garlic, chopped

¼ cup red wine vinegar

¾ cup chopped fresh basil, plus more for garnish

Toasted sunflower seeds, for garnish (optional)

Crackers, toast points, and/or cucumber slices, for serving

Prep time: 25 minutes

Cook time: 25 minutes

Makes 12 servings (about 6 cups)

1. Preheat the oven to 500°F. Line a baking sheet with foil.

2. Place the tomatoes whole on the prepared sheet. Roast for 10 minutes, turning once, until browned. Remove from the oven and set aside to cool.

3. Gently remove and discard the tomato skins and return the tomatoes to the foil. Holding on to the edges of the foil, carefully transfer the tomatoes and their juices to a blender or food processor. Pulse lightly until the mixture is puréed but still slightly chunky. Set aside.

4. Season the eggplants with the salt and black pepper.

5. In a large, heavy stockpot over medium heat, warm the oil. Add the eggplants, peppers, fennel, onion, and garlic and sauté for 15 minutes, until the eggplants and fennel begin to soften and brown.

6. Add the puréed tomatoes and red wine vinegar to the stockpot. Reduce the heat to medium–low, cover, and simmer, stirring occasionally, for 10 minutes, until the eggplant and onion are very tender. If any excess liquid remains, remove the cover and continue to cook until it has evaporated. Remove from the heat and stir in the ¾ cup of basil.

7. Transfer the caponata to a large serving bowl. Garnish with the sunflower seeds (if using) and extra basil. Serve warm, at room temperature, or cold with the crackers, toast points and/or cucumber slices. The caponata can be made up to 2 days ahead, covered, and chilled.

Goat Cheese Bruschetta with Arrabbiata Sauce and Poached Egg

My friends and I created a guys' cooking club called the Yo Yo Brotherhood. Once, we made a lentil and greens salad topped with poached eggs. It became the inspiration for this recipe, because we have realized that just about every dish can be improved with a gently poached farm-fresh egg. Of course, a good-quality local goat cheese, such as that from Capriole Farms, is also key, as it cools down the slightly spicy tomato sauce. Eggs sunny-side up or over easy would also work with this dish, as long as you get that runny yolk. —**Rick Turley, customer**

4 slices oval crusty bread, such as sourdough (about 4 inches in diameter)

5 ounces fresh goat cheese, room temperature

1 tablespoon olive oil

⅓ cup finely diced onion

5 cloves garlic, minced

⅛ teaspoon crushed red pepper flakes, plus more to taste

1½ cups diced fresh ripe tomatoes

Salt, to taste

Freshly ground black pepper, to taste

1 tablespoon vinegar or lemon juice

4 large market-fresh eggs

Prep time: 15 minutes

Cook time: 10 minutes

Makes 4 servings

1. Grill or toast the bread and immediately spread the goat cheese over the toasted slices. Set aside.

2. In a large skillet over medium heat, warm the oil. Add the onion, garlic, and red pepper flakes to the skillet and sauté for 5 minutes. Add the tomatoes and sauté for 5 minutes, until thickened. Remove from the heat and season with the salt and black pepper.

3. In a large sauté pan, bring 3 inches of water to a boil. Stir in the vinegar. Crack each egg into a ramekin or custard cup and gently drop them into the boiling water. Simmer gently for 2 minutes, until the egg whites have set (longer if you do not want runny egg yolks). Remove from the heat.

4. Spoon the hot tomato sauce over the cheese-covered toast. Using a slotted spoon, transfer 1 poached egg onto each slice, atop the tomato sauce. Season with the salt and black pepper. Serve immediately.

Tilapia Ceviche with Corn and Seasonal Herbs

One night in June, 2013, we had the opportunity to cook at Growing Power Farm's anniversary party. Of course, it turned out to be almost 100 degrees outside, coupled with one of those summer thunderstorms. Our grill didn't like that too much. One of the dishes we prepared was a tilapia ceviche using fish the farm raised sustainably in an aquaculture system. The fish is spectacular. The tilapia is right out of the water, beautiful and clean-tasting, and perfect for a hot summer day or lighter meal. Pair this dish with a cold Midwestern beer, like Three Floyds' Gumballhead, or a chilled light white wine, such as albariño.
—**Randy Zweiban, chef, SRZ Consulting**

---

8 ounces tilapia fillets, thinly sliced*
½ teaspoon salt
¼ teaspoon freshly ground black pepper
¼ cup fresh lemon juice
¼ cup fresh lime juice
½ cup peeled, seeded, and finely diced cucumber
½ cup corn kernels, toasted until lightly browned in a dry skillet

¼ cup finely diced onion
¼ cup finely chopped fresh cilantro
¼ cup finely chopped fresh chives
¼ cup extra virgin olive oil
1 locally grown jalapeño or serrano pepper, seeded and finely chopped (optional)
Tortilla, terra, or vegetable chips, for serving

Prep time: 15 minutes
Chill time: 2 to 2½ hours
Makes 4 servings

1. Place the tilapia in a shallow glass, stainless steel, or other nonreactive dish. Season with the salt and black pepper and cover with the lemon and lime juices. Mix well. Cover and chill for 1½ to 2 hours, until the fish is opaque.

2. Add the cucumber, corn, onion, cilantro, chives, and oil. Add the jalapeño pepper (if using). Mix well and chill for 30 minutes to allow the flavors to blend. Serve chilled with tortilla, terra, or vegetable chips.

* If you prefer to serve the fish cooked in a more traditional way, pan sear each tilapia fillet for 1 to 2 minutes per side and marinate it in the lemon and lime juices for about 30 minutes before slicing and serving.

Squash Blossoms Stuffed with Goat Cheese

I had never cooked with squash blossoms, but when I saw some beautiful ones for sale at Green City Market, I had to give them a try. After looking at dozens of recipes on the Internet, I decided to combine several ideas with what I had on hand, along with some other Market finds, like Capriole Farms goat cheese. I like to serve these stuffed blossoms with warm marinara sauce, but they are just as delicious without. —**Alderman Michele Smith, customer**

---

8 squash blossoms

3 ounces soft goat cheese, room temperature

¼ cup shredded or finely diced Gruyère cheese

2 tablespoons sour cream

1–2 tablespoons chopped fresh chives

Sunflower or canola oil, for frying

⅔ cup all-purpose flour

½ cup cold beer

Prep time: 20 minutes

Cook time: 4 minutes per batch

Makes 4 servings (2 stuffed blossoms per serving)

1. Rinse the squash blossoms in cold water and allow them to drain on paper towels.

2. In a small bowl, combine the goat cheese, Gruyère, sour cream, and chives and mix well.

3. Gently open the squash blossoms and remove the stamen in the center. If a small zucchini is beginning to grow from the bottom of the blossom, leave it attached. Leave the stems on to make it easy to turn the squash blossoms with tongs when in the hot oil.

4. Using about 2 teaspoons of the cheese mixture, form an oval shape and fill one of the blossoms. Close up the leaves around the cheese. Repeat with the remainder of the blossoms.

5. In a heavy pan over medium heat, heat ½ inch of the oil.

6. While the oil is heating, in a medium bowl, whisk together the flour and beer, creating a smooth batter.

Continued

7. When the oil registers 350°F to 360°F on a candy or deep-fry thermometer, hold 1 stuffed squash blossom by the stem and dip it in the batter. Place the blossom in the pan. Repeat with the remaining blossoms, but do not crowd the pan; the blossoms should not touch each other. Cook for 2 minutes per side, until golden brown. Remove from the heat.

8. Using a slotted spoon or tongs, transfer the blossoms to a plate lined with paper towels. If necessary, repeat with any remaining blossoms.

9. Transfer the blossoms to a serving platter and serve warm.

Eggplant Bites

Eggplant comes into season during the height of summer, when you can find all sizes, shapes, and shades of the sumptuous aubergine. This recipe treats eggplant as it would the meat in meatballs. Shaped into patties and baked, these bites make a great vegetarian meal or side dish. I almost always serve them as my go-to hors d'oeuvre at potlucks or when entertaining at home, and they always disappear immediately.
—**Linda Calafiore, Green City Market founding member**

¼ cup olive oil

1 medium eggplant (1–1¼ lbs), peeled and cut into ½-inch cubes

½ cup grated Parmesan cheese

⅓ cup plain dry breadcrumbs

¼ cup chopped fresh parsley

Salt, to taste

Prep time: 20 minutes

Cook time: 3 minutes

Makes 4 to 6 appetizer servings

1. In a large, deep skillet or sauté pan, warm the oil over medium heat. Add the eggplant to the skillet and sauté, stirring often, for 10 minutes, until very tender. Remove from the heat and transfer to a medium bowl. Let stand for 10 minutes.

2. Preheat the broiler on high.

3. Add the remaining ingredients to the eggplant and mix well. Measure 2 level tablespoons of the eggplant mixture into your hands. Shape into a ball 1 to 1¼ inches in diameter, pressing hard so the mixture holds together. Repeat with the remaining mixture until you have made 16 balls.

4. Place the balls on the baking sheet and place it in the broiler 4 to 5 inches from the heat source. Broil 2 to 3 minutes, until browned, watching carefully to avoid scorching. Remove from the oven.

5. Transfer to a serving platter. Serve warm or at room temperature.

Creamy Corn Bisque with Corn Fritters

My zeal for corn takes me home to the state of Iowa. I can recall the days of our state fair as a child, holding a hot, buttery ear of sweet corn and hearing my father proclaim, "Iowa only grows three types of sweet corn: pretty good, real good, and darn good." Now, I buy Illinois corn at the Market for the restaurant and can honestly say it really is "darn good." This is a soup I make as often as I can during corn season. —**Michael Paulsen, chef/owner, Abigail's American Bistro**

FOR THE CORN STOCK AND SOUP:

6 ears fresh sweet corn
1 small leek, white and light green parts, thinly sliced
2 shallots, thinly sliced
½ bulb fennel, chopped
1 small onion, chopped
2 cloves garlic, chopped
1 fresh bay leaf
½ teaspoon whole fennel seed
½ teaspoon whole coriander seed
½ teaspoon salt, plus more to taste
½ teaspoon freshly ground black pepper, plus more to taste
1 bunch fresh thyme, divided
1 bunch fresh parsley, divided
1 cup heavy cream
¼ cup unsalted butter

FOR THE FRITTERS:

1 tablespoon olive oil
2½ cups fresh corn kernels (from about 3 ears of corn)
½ cup chopped onion
1 tablespoon minced garlic
½ teaspoon salt, divided
¼ teaspoon freshly ground black pepper
1⅔ cups all-purpose flour
½ cup yellow cornmeal
1½ teaspoons baking powder
1 teaspoon sugar
2 large eggs
1 cup whole milk
½ teaspoon chopped fresh thyme leaves, plus more for garnish (optional)
½ teaspoon Worcestershire sauce
¼ teaspoon hot pepper sauce
Canola oil, for frying

Prep time: 30 minutes
Cook time: 40 minutes
Makes 6 servings

TO MAKE THE CORN STOCK AND SOUP:

1. Remove the kernels from the corncobs with a sharp knife and reserve them. Scrape the corncobs with the back of the knife and reserve the "milk." Break the cobs in half and place them in a large stainless-steel saucepan.

Continued

2. Add the leek, shallots, fennel, onion, garlic, bay leaf, fennel seed, coriander seed, salt, and black pepper to the saucepan. Add ½ of the thyme and ½ of the parsley. Cover with water and bring to a boil over high heat. Reduce the heat to a simmer and cook for 30 minutes.

3. Strain the stock, discarding the cobs and vegetables. Return the stock to the saucepan over medium heat and add the reserved corn kernels, the cream, and the butter. Tie together the remaining thyme and parsley and add them to the saucepan. Bring to a gentle simmer and cook for 20 minutes. Remove from the heat and remove and discard the herbs.

4. Transfer the soup to a blender (you may need to work in batches) and blend until puréed. Strain the soup into a large bowl, pressing down on the solids to get as much liquid as possible. Discard the solids. Return the soup to the saucepan and season with the salt and black pepper.

TO MAKE THE FRITTERS:

1. In a medium skillet over medium heat, warm the oil. Add the corn, onion, garlic, ¼ teaspoon of the salt, and black pepper. Sauté for 3 minutes, until the corn is tender. Remove from the heat and set aside to cool.

2. In a medium bowl, combine the flour, cornmeal, baking powder, and sugar. Mix well and set aside.

3. In a large bowl, beat the eggs. Gradually add the milk, beating constantly. Stir in the flour mixture and combine until the dry ingredients are moistened. Stir in the thyme, Worcestershire sauce, and hot pepper sauce. Add the cooked corn mixture and stir well to combine until a batter forms.

4. In a medium saucepan over medium heat, warm 3 inches of the canola oil. When the oil registers 350°F on a candy or deep-fry thermometer, drop the batter into the saucepan by the tablespoonful. Cook in batches and do not crowd the fritters, or the oil's temperature will drop. When the fritters pop to the surface, roll them around with a slotted spoon to ensure that they fry evenly. Cook for 2 minutes, until golden brown. Remove from the heat and transfer to a plate lined with paper towels. Season with the remaining salt.

5. Reheat the soup and top with the fritters. Serve garnished with the fresh thyme leaves, if desired.

Roasted San Marzano Tomato Soup

I love making this soup because it is healthy and easy. When tomatoes are in season, I make it twice a week. Several vendors grow San Marzano tomatoes, which are ripest at the height of summer and have a sweet, "tomato-y" flavor. The soup may be prepared and refrigerated for up to 3 days or frozen for up to 3 months. —**Robin Goldberg, customer**

1 pound cherry tomatoes, halved

1¼ pounds ripe San Marzano tomatoes or plum tomatoes, halved lengthwise

3 large shallots, peeled and thinly sliced

2 tablespoons olive oil

1 tablespoon sugar

3 cups chicken broth or stock

Salt, to taste

Freshly ground black pepper, to taste

½ cup heavy cream or half and half (optional)

Chopped fresh basil, for garnish (optional)

Prep time: 20 minutes

Cook time: 1 hour 5 minutes

Makes 4 servings

1. Preheat the oven to 300°F.

2. On a large rimmed baking sheet, arrange the tomatoes and shallots in a single layer. Drizzle the oil and sprinkle the sugar evenly over the tomatoes and shallots. Bake for 45 minutes, until very tender. Remove from the oven.

3. Pour the tomato mixture and its juices into a large saucepan over high heat (use a rubber spatula to make sure you get everything). Add the broth and bring to a boil. Reduce the heat to medium–low and allow the mixture to reach a gentle simmer. Simmer for 20 minutes and remove from the heat.

4. Using an immersion blender or a conventional blender, purée the soup to a smooth texture. You may wish to let the soup cool a bit before transferring it to a blender.

5. Pour the soup through a fine mesh strainer to remove any small pieces of skin and seeds. Discard the solids. Season with the salt and black pepper. Stir in the cream (if desired).

6. Reheat the soup and serve garnished with the basil (if desired).

Summer Bean Salad with Sun Gold Tomatoes, Market Herbs, Smoked Trout, and Goat Cheese Dressing

I've been going to Green City Market twice a week since 1999. My thing is to get there before anybody else, just before it opens—around 6:00 a.m. At that hour, I might chance upon a special find or something in limited quantity—tiny mustard greens with flowers, baby sunchokes, or the first of the July tomatoes. The beans and tomatoes in this dish just happened to be sitting on Beth Eccles's tables at the Green Acres Farm stand one day, and the idea leapt into my mind to do a light salad with smoked trout from Rushing Waters. These are the kinds of magical moments you search for as a chef—those that seem to happen at that early-morning hour as you walk through the day's harvest. —**Jason Hammel, co-owner/chef, Lula Café; co-owner, Nightwood Restaurant**

2¼ teaspoons salt, divided

½ pound mixed pole beans, such as yellow, green, and haricots verts, etc.

2 small pattypan squash, sliced on a mandoline or very thinly sliced

2 radishes, sliced on a mandoline or very thinly sliced

½ cup yellow Sun Gold cherry tomatoes, quartered or halved

2 tablespoons extra virgin olive oil

2 teaspoons red wine vinegar or champagne vinegar

¼ cup chopped mixed fresh herbs, such as tarragon, thyme, basil, and chives

¼ cup sour cream

¼ cup buttermilk

1 small shallot, minced

1 tablespoon honey

1½ teaspoons cider vinegar

1 teaspoon Dijon mustard

½ cup crumbled goat cheese

3 ounces smoked trout, broken into chunks

Prep time: 30 minutes

Cook time: 1 minute

Makes 4 servings

1. Place a bowl of ice water next to the sink.

2. Fill a large stockpot with water and place it over high heat. Add 2 teaspoons of the salt and bring to a rolling boil. Add the beans and simmer for 30 seconds to 1 minute. Remove from the heat.

3. Drain the beans and plunge them into the ice water bath to cool. Drain, pat dry with a paper towel, and cut the beans on the bias into ½-inch slices.

4. In a large bowl, toss together the beans, squash, radishes, tomatoes, oil, red wine vinegar, and the remaining ¼ teaspoon of salt. Add the herbs and toss again.

5. In a medium bowl, combine the sour cream, buttermilk, shallot, honey, cider vinegar, and mustard and mix well. Stir in the goat cheese.

6. Spoon the dressing onto 4 serving plates. Top with the bean mixture and smoked trout and serve.

Peach and Tomato Panzanella Salad

At Purple Asparagus, a nonprofit organization that educates children, families, and the community about healthful, sustainable food, we teach recipes that use produce in unique and inviting ways. Green City Market is often my inspiration for these recipes. In this dish, I combine the best of summer's fruits—sweet peaches, tart tomatoes, and crunchy cucumbers—in a way that appeals to parents and kids alike. Kids can easily tackle each of the recipe's steps: mixing the dressing, tearing the bread, cutting the fruit, tearing the basil, and, of course, tossing it all together. It's a welcome addition to any family table. —**Melissa Graham, volunteer**

---

2 tablespoons extra virgin olive oil

2 teaspoons balsamic vinegar

½ teaspoon sea salt

3 cups fresh bread cubes (your favorite Green City Market bread, with crust, cut into ½-inch cubes)

1 medium cucumber, peeled (if desired) and cut into ½-inch cubes

2 cups diced ripe tomatoes, preferably a mix of yellow and red tomatoes

1 ripe peach, cut into ½-inch cubes

¼ cup packed fresh basil leaves

Prep time: 20 minutes

Makes 4 to 6 servings

1. In a large serving bowl, whisk together the oil, vinegar, and salt. Add the bread, cucumber, tomatoes, and peach and toss lightly.

2. Tear the basil into small pieces and add it to the salad. Toss again until well combined. Serve immediately.

Heirloom Tomato Salad with Aged Cheddar

This recipe is adapted from a salad I enjoyed at Meritage Café & Wine Bar, which has since closed. It lends itself beautifully to the peak of Green City Market's heirloom tomato season. Choose different colored tomatoes for an even more beautiful presentation. The cheese is the finishing touch! —**Laura Sterkel, volunteer**

6 assorted heirloom tomatoes, sliced

½ cup packed baby arugula

½ cup shredded 3-year-aged Cheddar cheese

3 strips uncured bacon, cooked crisp and crumbled (optional)

2 tablespoons extra virgin olive oil

2 teaspoons balsamic vinegar

Salt, to taste

Freshly ground black pepper, to taste

Prep time: 20 minutes

Makes 4 servings

1. Arrange the tomatoes onto 4 serving plates. Top with the arugula, cheese, and bacon (if desired). Drizzle the oil and vinegar over the salads. Season with the salt and black pepper and serve.

Broccoli and Mushroom Salad

This is a popular recipe at our family barbecues. The bright green broccoli pairs well with the earthy mushrooms, which pick up a sweet-and-sour flavor from the dressing. I find Green City Market broccoli to have a milder, fresher taste and to be much more tender than the grocery store version. —**Audrey Miller, customer**

⅓ cup olive oil
3 tablespoons cider vinegar
1 tablespoon Dijon mustard
1 tablespoon brown sugar
1 clove garlic, put through a garlic press

1 large bunch broccoli (about 1¼ pounds), cut into florets (reserving the stalk for another use)
½ cup finely diced red bell pepper
8 ounces fresh cremini, oyster, and/or other mushrooms, sliced

Prep time: 15 minutes

Chill time: 8 hours or overnight

Makes 8 servings

1. In a small bowl, whisk together the oil, vinegar, mustard, sugar, and garlic. Set aside.

2. In a medium serving bowl, combine the broccoli and red bell pepper. Add the dressing and toss well. Chill for at least 8 hours or overnight.

3. Just before serving, add the mushrooms and toss well.

Watermelon, Arugula, and Feta Salad

I love this recipe (adapted from chef Ina Garten's version) because it is a tasty and easy dish to make for a group, either when dining at home or when preparing for a picnic. The contrast in flavors between the sweet watermelon and sharp feta is delicious, and the peppery arugula is the icing on the cake. When I see the first melons appear at the Market, I know summer has arrived, and it's time for fun parties and picnics! —**Adrienne Lawrence, customer**

2 tablespoons orange juice

1 tablespoon honey

2 tablespoons olive oil

¼ whole watermelon, rind removed, cut into
    1-inch cubes (6 cups)

8 ounces feta cheese, broken into ½-inch pieces

2 cups packed baby arugula

½ cup sliced fresh apricots (optional)

½ cup packed whole mint leaves,
    cut into thin strips

Freshly ground black pepper, to taste

Prep time: 25 minutes

Makes 6 to 8 servings
(about 8 cups)

1. In a small bowl, combine the orange juice and honey. Gradually whisk in the oil until thickened. If not using this dressing within 1 hour, chill until ready to use.

2. In a large serving bowl, combine the watermelon, cheese, arugula, and apricots (if desired). Drizzle the dressing over the salad and toss lightly. Add the mint and black pepper, and toss again. Serve immediately.

Grilled Portobello Steak and Potato Salad

I once overheard someone say, "Nobody makes friends over salad." This recipe is my response to this statement. Not only will you make friends, you will also make friends for life—maybe even lovers! This is the mother of all salads—a steakhouse version with plenty of delicious summertime vegetables, but without the meat. —**Jacqueline Fisch, customer**

2 large or 3 medium portobello mushrooms, cleaned, stems trimmed

2 tablespoons red or white wine

2 tablespoons balsamic vinegar

Salt, to taste

Freshly ground black pepper, to taste

3 cups cubed scrubbed potatoes (about ¾-inch chunks)

3 tablespoons olive oil, divided

1 small yellow or white onion, sliced

1 medium yellow squash or zucchini, diagonally cut into ¼-inch slices

½ cup grilled corn kernels (cut from 1 ear of grilled corn) (optional)

1 large roasted red bell pepper (bottled is okay)

1 tablespoon fresh lemon juice

1 teaspoon prepared horseradish

4 cups packed mixed baby or torn salad greens

Chopped fresh parsley, for garnish (optional)

Prep time: 40 minutes

Cook time: 20 minutes

Makes 4 servings

1. Preheat the oven to 400°F.

2. If desired, scrape out the dark gills from the undersides of the mushrooms with a spoon.

3. Place the mushrooms on a shallow plate and drizzle the wine and vinegar over them. Turn the mushrooms over and season them with the salt and black pepper. (They will absorb most of the marinade.) Set aside and let stand at room temperature while preparing the potatoes.

4. In a large bowl, toss the potatoes with 1 tablespoon of the oil.

5. Transfer the potatoes to a rimmed baking sheet or roasting pan and arrange them in a single layer. Season with the salt and black pepper and roast in the oven for 10 minutes. Toss well and continue to roast for 10 to 12 minutes, until browned and tender. Remove from the oven and set aside.

Continued

6. In a large skillet over medium heat, heat 1 tablespoon of the oil. Add the onion and zucchini and sauté for 8 to 10 minutes, until tender. Remove from the heat and stir in the corn (if desired). Transfer the mixture to a bowl and cover with foil to keep warm.

7. Add the mushrooms to the same skillet over medium heat and sauté for 3 to 4 minutes per side, until lightly browned and tender. Remove from the heat and set aside.

8. Place the roasted pepper, lemon juice, horseradish, and the remaining 1 tablespoon of oil in a blender or the bowl of a mini food processor. Process until puréed. Season with the salt and black pepper and set aside.

9. Arrange the greens on 4 serving plates. Slice the mushrooms thickly and arrange them over the greens. Arrange the potatoes and onion–zucchini mixture over the mushrooms. Drizzle the dressing over the salads, garnish with the parsley, and serve.

Sunset Salad with Beets, Plums, and Tomatoes

This salad really means summer in Chicago to me—it is the perfect addition to a late-harvest meal after a trip to the Market. It also celebrates local growers, who have rescued so many heirloom varieties of tomatoes and plums. They're at their best at this season and complement each other in flavor and color. —**Judith Dunbar Hines, customer**

4 medium golden beets, trimmed and
    quartered
4 fresh plums, pitted and cut into ½-inch slices
1 cup yellow pear or cherry tomatoes, halved
2 tablespoons olive oil
2 tablespoons red wine vinegar

1 tablespoon finely chopped chives
1 teaspoon chopped thyme leaves
1 teaspoon Dijon mustard
½ teaspoon salt
¼ teaspoon freshly ground black pepper
3 cups mixed baby salad greens

Prep time: 20 minutes
Cook time: 1 hour
Makes 4 to 6 servings

1. Preheat the oven to 450°F.

2. In a large, deep baking dish, place the beets and about 1 inch of water. Cover tightly with foil. Bake for 1 hour, until the beets are very tender. Remove from the oven and cool to room temperature.

3. Place the plums and tomatoes in a large bowl. Slice the beets into chunks and set aside.

4. In a medium jar with a tight-fitting lid, combine the oil, vinegar, chives, thyme, mustard, salt, and black pepper. Shake well. Pour ½ of the dressing over the plum mixture.

5. Add the beets to the bowl. Toss well and let stand for 15 minutes.

6. Arrange the greens on 4 to 6 serving plates. Drizzle with more of the dressing and top with the beet mixture.

Cauliflower Cake

Cauliflower is often overlooked in late summer, when so many colorful fruits and vegetables abound, but its white florets are sweet and delicious this time of year. This savory cake makes a nice side dish for grilled meats, a dramatic centerpiece for vegetarian dinners, or a fine luncheon star when served with a salad. —**Judith Stockdale, customer**

1 medium head cauliflower, cut into medium florets
1 large red onion
⅓ cup olive oil
½ teaspoon minced fresh rosemary leaves
8 large eggs
1½ cups all-purpose flour

2½ teaspoons baking powder
½ teaspoon ground turmeric
1½ teaspoons salt
½ teaspoon freshly ground black pepper
¼ cup chopped fresh basil leaves
2 cups finely grated Wisconsin Parmesan cheese
Unsalted butter, for greasing

Prep time: 55 minutes
Cook time: 45 minutes
Makes 6 to 8 servings

1. Preheat the oven to 350°F.

2. In a large stockpot of salted water over medium heat, simmer the cauliflower for 15 minutes, until soft but not mushy. Remove from the heat. Drain, rinse with cold water, and drain again in a colander.

3. Cut several thin slices from one end of the onion. Separate into rings and set aside. Coarsely chop the rest of the onion.

4. In a large skillet over medium heat, warm the oil. Add the chopped onion and rosemary and sauté until the onion has softened, about 8 minutes. Remove from the heat and set aside to cool.

5. In a medium bowl, combine the flour, baking powder, turmeric, salt and pepper. Set aside.

6. In a large bowl, whisk the eggs. Add the cooled onion mixture and the basil. Whisk in the flour mixture. Stir in the cheese until well combined. Stir in the cauliflower. Set aside.

7. Thoroughly grease the inside of a 9-inch springform pan. Line the bottom with parchment paper and grease the paper. Pour the cauliflower mixture into the pan. Arrange the reserved onion rings attractively over the top.

8. Bake for 45 to 50 minutes, until the cake is golden brown and the center is set. Remove from the oven. Run a thin spatula or knife around the edges of the pan. Let stand for 10 minutes. Remove the rim of the pan before cutting the cake into wedges. Serve warm or at room temperature.

Goat Burger with Shallot Aioli and Okra Relish

In the Midwest, our unpredictable produce seasons make every trip to Green City Market fun! You never know what will be available. It's also fun to chat with farmers about what's around and what might be coming soon. Green City Market is also great for just wandering around and finding new things to use in cooking—like okra. I never knew I loved okra until we tried grilling some from Nichols Farm & Orchard. Now I text Nick Nichols in the beginning of the season to ask when the okra will be ready! Char grilling, rather than sautéing or steaming, helps prevent the okra from becoming slimy. And, of course, I love working with goat meat from our local farmers. Over the past three years, we have tried just about everything with goat...maybe because of the restaurant's name? But a burger is an easy way to enjoy the meat, pure and simple. —**Stephanie Izard, executive chef, Girl & the Goat, Little Goat Diner**

FOR THE SHALLOT AIOLI (MAKES ABOUT ¾ CUP):

3 tablespoons minced shallots

1 tablespoon Dijon mustard

1 egg yolk

1 clove garlic, minced

1 teaspoon Worcestershire sauce

1 teaspoon fresh lemon juice

½ cup grapeseed or canola oil, plus more if needed

Salt, to taste

Freshly ground black pepper, to taste

FOR THE OKRA RELISH (MAKES ABOUT 1½ CUPS):

1 pound fresh okra

2 tablespoons plus 1 teaspoon extra virgin olive oil, divided

⅛ teaspoon salt

⅛ teaspoon freshly ground black pepper

1 large poblano pepper

2 tablespoons malt or rice vinegar

1 large shallot, minced

FOR THE GOAT BURGERS:

2 pounds ground goat meat

½ teaspoon salt

½ teaspoon freshly ground black pepper

4 soft sesame seed or pretzel buns, grilled or toasted, for serving

1 large heirloom tomato, cut into 4 slices for serving

Prep time: 40 minutes

Cook time: 10 minutes

Makes 4 servings

TO MAKE THE SHALLOT AIOLI:

1. In a small bowl, whisk together the shallots, mustard, egg yolk, garlic, Worcestershire sauce, and lemon juice. Gradually whisk in the oil. Season with the salt and black pepper. Set aside.

TO MAKE THE OKRA RELISH:

1. Preheat the grill to medium–high (350°F to 400°F).

2. In a large bowl, toss the okra with 1 teaspoon of the oil, the salt, and the black pepper. Place the okra on the grill and cook for 2 to 3 minutes per side, until charred. Remove from the grill and set aside to cool.

3. Cut the cooled okra into ¼-inch slices. Set aside.

4. On the grill or on a gas burner, char the poblano pepper until its skin is blistered. Remove from the grill. Wrap the pepper in foil and let cool for 5 minutes. Remove and discard the skin. Stem and peel the pepper and cut it into ¼-inch pieces. Set aside.

5. In a small bowl, whisk together the vinegar and the remaining 2 tablespoons of the oil. Stir in the okra, poblano pepper, and shallot. Set aside.

TO MAKE THE GOAT BURGERS:

1. Divide the meat into 4 portions. Without overhandling the meat, form each portion into a ½-inch-thick patty. Season with the salt and black pepper.

2. Place the burgers on the grill and cook for 5 minutes per side for medium doneness. Remove from the grill.

3. Serve the burgers in the buns, topped with the tomato slices, Okra Relish, and Shallot Aioli.

Note: This recipe uses raw egg. Cases of salmonella poisoning have been traced to raw eggs, although this is rare.

Tofu Stir Fry with Ginger and Bell Peppers

This dish could be called Grandma Yang's Tofu because it's a variation on a recipe my mom used to cook when I was young. As we got older, the recipe got a little spicier, and I decided to make it a little spicier still. I've always enjoyed sharing this with our customers because it brings me a lot of good memories of my youth. We make our cholesterol-, gluten-, and preservative-free tofu by hand each week, in small batches. We use filtered water and non-GMO soybeans grown in Illinois without the use of chemicals, pesticides, or fungicides.

—Jenny Yang, vendor, Phoenix Bean

2 tablespoons olive oil

1 red bell pepper, cut into thin slices

1 tablespoon minced fresh ginger

1 clove garlic, minced

1 (14-ounce) package fresh extra-firm
    tofu, diced

¼ cup water

1 teaspoon ground turmeric

3 tablespoons soy sauce

2 green onions, thinly sliced on the bias

Prep time: 10 minutes

Cook time: 11 minutes

Makes 4 servings

1. In a wok or large skillet over medium heat, warm the oil. Add the red pepper, ginger, and garlic and stir fry for 2 to 3 minutes.

2. Add the tofu and water to the wok and stir fry for 3 to 4 minutes, until heated through. Add the turmeric and stir fry for 1 minute. Add the soy sauce and stir fry for 2 to 3 minutes, until the sauce thickens. Remove from the heat.

3. Transfer the mixture to 4 serving plates. Top with the green onions and serve.

Wild Mushroom Pasta with Sweet Corn and Bacon

I served this dish at our very first Pasta Puttana dinner. The event was too dark, too hot, and it entirely lacked seating (note: I've since improved upon the atmosphere of our dinners), but this summertime pasta dish made it all worthwhile. The combination of raw sweet corn, salty bacon, and earthy mushroom pasta is magical. Jars of our Peppadew peppers are available at our shop, but you can also substitute ½ cup of sliced, freshly roasted red bell peppers or bottled roasted red peppers. —**Jessica Volpe, vendor, Pasta Puttana**

---

2 slices slab bacon or 4 ounces bacon ends, cut into 1-inch lardons

1 ear fresh sweet corn kernels, removed from the cob

4 bottled red Peppadew peppers, sliced

1 (8-ounce) bag fresh wild mushroom pasta, tagliatelle, or pappardelle, as desired

2 quarts salted water

1 tablespoon butternut squash seed oil or extra virgin olive oil

2 tablespoons chopped fresh herbs, such as basil, chives, or parsley

---

Prep time: 15 minutes

Cook time: 6 minutes

Makes 2 servings

1. In a large skillet over medium heat, cook the lardons for 5 to 6 minutes, turning occasionally, until lightly browned. Remove from the heat. Transfer to a paper towel, reserving the drippings in the skillet. Set aside.

2. In a large bowl, combine the corn and peppers. Set aside.

3. In a medium bowl, place the pasta and toss gently with your hands to separate.

4. To a large stockpot over medium–high heat, add the water and bring to a boil. Add the pasta, stirring immediately so the strands cook evenly. Cook for 30 to 45 seconds, stirring once more. Remove from the heat and drain.

5. Place the pasta in the large bowl over the corn and peppers. Let stand 1 minute to allow the mixture to heat through.

6. Add the lardons, 1 tablespoon of the lardon drippings, and the oil. Toss gently.

7. Transfer the pasta to 2 serving plates and top with the herbs. Serve warm.

Grilled Fish Tacos with Tomatillo Salsa

My kind of summer recipe is one where everything can be sourced from Green City Market, and this recipe—with the addition of a few pantry staples—fits the bill. I love this classic tomatillo salsa with walleye, but it works with plenty of other fish, too, not to mention steak or chicken, or mixed into guacamole. —**Rick Bayless, co-owner/chef, Frontera Grill, Topolobampo, XOCO; Green City Market founding member**

FOR THE FISH:

3 cloves garlic, peeled

1 large white onion, thickly sliced, divided

3 tablespoons fresh lime juice

½ teaspoon ground cumin

½ teaspoon salt

4 walleye pike fish fillets, with skin
   (about 1½ pounds)

FOR THE TOMATILLO SALSA:

8 ounces fresh tomatillos, husked

1 serrano or jalapeño chile pepper, stemmed
   and, if desired, seeded

¼ cup coarsely chopped white onion

½ cup chopped fresh cilantro, divided

¼ teaspoon salt

FOR COOKING AND SERVING:

Oil, for brushing

Lime wedges, for serving

12 fresh corn tortillas, warmed, for serving

Prep time: 30 minutes

Cook time: 8 minutes

Chill time: 1 to 2 hours

Makes 4 servings

TO MAKE THE FISH:

1. Using a food processor with the motor running, drop the garlic through the feed tube and process until minced. Add 1 slice of the onion, the lime juice, the cumin, and the salt and process to a smooth purée. Stop the processor motor. Transfer the marinade to a bowl and set aside.

2. Oil the skin sides of the fish. Place them, skin side down, into a glass baking dish. Spread the marinade over the fish. Cover and chill for 1 to 2 hours.

Continued

TO MAKE THE TOMATILLO SALSA:

1. In a large saucepan over medium–high heat, place the tomatillos and cover with water. Salt the water and bring to a boil. Cook for 6 to 8 minutes, until the tomatillos are almost tender. Remove from the heat. Drain and cool in cold water.

2. Using a food processor, pulse the chile pepper until it is minced. Add the tomatillos, the onion, ¼ cup of the cilantro, and the salt and process to a coarse purée. Transfer to a serving dish and set aside.

TO COOK AND SERVE:

1. Preheat the grill to medium–high (350°F to 400°F).

2. Brush both sides of the remaining onion slices (from the fish preparation) with the oil.

3. Remove the fish from the marinade and shake gently to drain any remaining marinade. Oil the fish well on both sides. Place the fish and onion slices on the grill together and cook for 4 minutes per side, turning once, until the onion slices are lightly browned and fish is almost flaking. Remove from the grill.

4. Break the fish into large pieces, removing and discarding the skin. Place on a warmed platter. Top with the grilled onions and remaining cilantro. Serve with the Tomatillo Salsa, lime wedges, and tortillas for your guests to make into soft tacos.

Grilled Skirt Steaks with Green Beans, Tomatoes, and Pesto

When shopping at the Market in the summer, I make it a point to pick up those lovely green beans, tomatoes, and some fresh basil pesto. To combine all these ingredients, I picked up some steaks from Heartland Meats and used a recipe I cut out of Gourmet *magazine years ago. This is my version of a simple but very tasty summer recipe.* —**Harriet Rosenman, customer**

3 cloves garlic, put through a garlic press
1–1¼ pounds skirt steak, cut into 4 pieces
½ teaspoon salt
½ teaspoon freshly ground black pepper

1 pound fresh thin green beans
½ cup prepared basil pesto
2 cups seeded and diced ripe tomatoes

Prep time: 15 minutes
Cook time: 10 minutes
Makes 4 servings

1. Preheat the grill to medium–high (350°F to 400°F).

2. Spread the garlic over the steaks and sprinkle with the salt and black pepper.

3. Place the steaks on the grill and cook for 3 minutes per side for thin steaks or 4 to 5 minutes per side for thicker steaks, for medium rare. Remove from the grill and let rest, tented with foil, for 5 minutes before serving.

4. Bring a large pot of salted water over medium heat to a simmer. Add the beans and cook for 4 minutes, until crisp-tender. Remove from the heat, drain well, and transfer to a medium bowl.

5. Add the pesto to the bowl and toss well. Add the tomatoes and toss again.

6. Arrange the beans on 4 serving plates and top with the steaks. Serve warm.

Sunday Dinner Club Market Burger

We really deeply love a good burger. Sunday Dinner Club has always served up the foods we crave using the best ingredients we can find. We like our burgers simple, but each component is carefully sourced and handled. Over the years at Green City Market, we've made many friends who have sought out a weekly burger from our stand while shopping the Market. One group remains our favorite—all of the farmers who line up at 7 a.m., just as the grill is getting fired up, to order a burger for what might appear to be a hearty breakfast and fuel for the long day. The truth is that these farmers rose at 2 a.m. to drive hours to Chicago for the early morning Market, so really, our hamburgers are their lunch. —**Joshua Kulp and Christine Cikowski, chefs/co-owners, Sunday Dinner Club and Honey Butter Fried Chicken**

FOR THE ROASTED GARLIC MAYO:

1 head garlic
2 teaspoons olive oil
1 cup mayonnaise
Juice from ½ lemon
Kosher salt, to taste
Freshly ground black pepper, to taste

FOR THE BURGERS:

2 pounds ground beef chuck*
6 soft New England, challah, or pretzel
    hamburger buns
Brunkow Cheese's Horseradish Cheddar
    Spread (or similar spread), to taste
Ketchup and mustard, such as LocalFolks
    Foods brand (optional)
1 bunch arugula

Prep time: 30 minutes

Cook time:
    garlic, 30 minutes
    burgers, 8 minutes

Makes 6 servings

TO MAKE THE ROASTED GARLIC MAYO:

1. Preheat the oven to 350°F.

2. Cut the top off the head of garlic, place it on a small sheet of foil, and drizzle it with the oil. Wrap the foil around the garlic and bake it for 30 minutes, until soft and golden brown. Remove from the oven and allow it to cool completely.

3. Squeeze the garlic from the skins and discard the skins. Mash the garlic into a paste. Place the mashed garlic in a small bowl and add the mayonnaise; mix well. Add the lemon juice and season with the salt and black pepper. Stir well. Refrigerate until ready to serve (will keep for up to 4 days).

Continued

TO MAKE THE BURGERS:

1. Divide the beef into 6 portions gently shaped into loose balls. Gently press each ball into a patty of the desired thickness, taking care not to overwork the beef.

2. Preheat a charcoal grill with hot coals using lump wood natural charcoal, started using a chimney (and not lighter fluid). Allow the grates to heat up.

3. Place the beef patties on the grill and cook for 2 to 3 minutes on 1 side, until seared. Once the meat releases easily or has a good sear, turn to the other side and cook for 2 minutes, to medium rare (or longer to desired doneness). Remove from the grill.

4. Place the bottoms of the buns on a serving platter and spread the Roasted Garlic Mayo on them. Place the burgers on the bottoms of the buns and spread the Horseradish Cheddar Spread on the tops of the buns. Add the ketchup and mustard, if using, and top the burgers with the arugula. Place the bun tops on the burgers and serve warm.

* If you choose to grind your own meat or have a local butcher do the grinding, look for an ideal meat-to-fat ratio of about 80/20, and consider adding short rib or brisket to the mix. Grind the beef fresh the day you are going to serve it. Make sure the beef is super cold, or perhaps even a little frozen, before you grind it. Remove any gristle or silverskin from the beef. Cut the beef into pieces that will fit through your grinder, season it with salt and black pepper, and use a medium die on your grinder to gently push the beef through.

Grilled Whitefish with Blueberry Salsa

My family loves trying different kinds of salsa. I first made this version after buying blueberries from the Market in the summer. Everyone loved it, and I know we will make it every season for years to come. The salsa really perks up simply grilled Great Lakes whitefish fillets from Jake's Country Meats, but it is also great served as an appetizer with tortilla chips.
—**Karen Theis, customer**

FOR THE BLUEBERRY SALSA:

1 cup chopped blueberries

1 cup whole blueberries

½ cup finely diced red bell pepper

¼ cup thinly sliced green onion or chopped white onion

2 tablespoons chopped cilantro

1 small jalapeño pepper, seeded, minced

1 tablespoon fresh lemon juice

1 tablespoon olive oil (optional)

¼ teaspoon coarse sea salt or kosher salt

FOR THE FISH:

2 (8-ounce) whitefish fillets with skin

1 tablespoon olive oil

½ teaspoon coarse sea salt or kosher salt

¼ teaspoon freshly ground black pepper

Prep time: 15 minutes

Cook time: 8 minutes

Makes 4 servings

TO MAKE THE BLUEBERRY SALSA:

1. Combine all the ingredients in a medium bowl. Cover and chill until serving time.

TO MAKE THE FISH:

1. Preheat the grill to medium–high (350°F to 400°F).

2. Brush both sides of the fish with the oil and season with the salt and black pepper. Place the fish on the grill, skin side down, and cook, covered, for 7 to 8 minutes, until the fish is opaque in the center. Remove from the grill.

3. Cut each fillet in half and place on a warmed plate. Top each piece of fish with some of the Blueberry Salsa. Any remaining salsa may be refrigerated up to two days.

Iron Creek Ratatouille

Ratatouille is a favorite dish in our family. Using fresh-picked ingredients from our farm, we enjoy this delicious and easy recipe all summer long, after the tomatoes have had a good head start in our greenhouse. Leftovers will keep in the refrigerator up to 4 days.
—**Tamera Mark, farmer, Iron Creek Farm**

2 tablespoons olive oil

1 small onion, chopped (1 cup)

1 small eggplant, unpeeled, cut into ½-inch cubes (2 cups)

1 large red bell pepper, cut into ½-inch cubes (2 cups)

1 large zucchini, cut into ½-inch cubes (2 cups)

2 cups ripe tomatoes, peeled if desired, cut into ½-inch cubes

¼ cup packed fresh basil leaves, chopped

Salt, to taste

Freshly ground black pepper, to taste

Prep time: 20 minutes

Cook time: 20 minutes

Makes 4 to 6 servings

1. In a large, deep skillet or sauté pan over medium heat, warm the oil. Add the onion and eggplant and sauté for 5 minutes.

2. Add the red bell pepper and squash to the skillet and sauté for 10 minutes. Add the tomatoes and sauté for 5 minutes, until the vegetables are tender. Remove from the heat.

3. Stir in the basil and season with the salt and black pepper. Transfer to a serving bowl and serve warm or at room temperature.

Confetti Corn

After the Fourth of July, you can always count on an abundance of fresh corn to pour into the Market. This is also when the farmers bring in tons of colorful peppers. I love this recipe because it takes advantage of both of these wonderful vegetables at the height of summer. I love to use Mirai corn for its sweetness, and colorful peppers from Leaning Shed Farm or Nichols Farm & Orchard. If you are using the bacon, try Jake's Country Meats. The fresh herbs from Smits Farms are always excellent. And, of course, I always use the delicious Summer Butter from Nordic Creamery; it makes everything that much better! —**Jill Remenar, customer**

2 tablespoons organic unsalted butter

2 cups diced mixed bell peppers, such as red, green, and purple

⅔ cup chopped red or yellow onion

4 cups sweet corn kernels (from 4 to 6 ears, depending on size)

½ teaspoon salt

¼ teaspoon freshly ground black pepper

¼ cup chopped fresh herbs, such as basil, chives, or parsley

4 slices bacon, cooked, crumbled (optional)

Prep time: 15 minutes

Cook time: 10 minutes

Makes 6 servings

1. In a large skillet over medium heat, melt the butter. Add the bell peppers and onion and sauté for 5 minutes.

2. Add the corn to the skillet and sauté for 3 to 4 minutes, until the corn is heated through. Remove from the heat. Season with the salt and black pepper. Stir in the herbs and the bacon, if using.

3. Transfer the dish to a serving bowl and serve hot.

Seasonal Vegetable-Stuffed Zucchini

The excellence of stuffed zucchini depends on the bounty of the seasonal Market, with its bunches of sweet onions and rows of celery, sweet peppers, tomatoes, and herbs. These basic ingredients are easily enhanced by a variety of mushrooms or Italian sausage, with the zucchini baked in the oven or prepared on a grill. As an accompaniment to a steak or chops, this recipe, adapted from my book Oysters: A Culinary Celebration, *is both savory and sassy.* —**Joan Reardon, customer**

---

3 large zucchini, about 2 inches in diameter
2 tablespoons olive oil
½ cup finely chopped cremini or button
   mushrooms
¼ cup finely chopped sweet onion
¼ cup finely chopped celery
¼ cup finely chopped red bell pepper

¼ cup chopped, seeded tomato
¼ cup chopped fresh herbs, such as basil,
   parsley, chives and thyme
Salt, to taste
Freshly ground black pepper, to taste
½ cup fresh breadcrumbs

Prep time: 25 minutes

Cook time: 15 minutes

Makes 6 servings

1. Preheat the oven to 350°F.

2. Trim the ends of the zucchini and cut it crosswise into 2-inch pieces. Using a melon baller or spoon, remove the center from each slice, leaving a ¼-inch shell on the bottom and sides that forms a cup to hold the stuffing. Finely chop the pulp and set it aside.

3. Bring a large pot of salted water over medium–high heat to a boil. Use a strainer or slotted spoon to place ¼ of the zucchini shells into the water and simmer for 1 to 2 minutes. Remove from the heat. Using a strainer or spider, transfer the shells to a bowl of ice water. Repeat with the remaining shells. Drain the shells and invert them onto a plate lined with paper towels or other absorbent paper.

4. In a large skillet over medium heat, warm the oil. Add the zucchini pulp and the remaining vegetables to the skillet and sauté for 5 to 6 minutes, until they are tender and the juices are reduced. Add the herbs and sauté for 1 minute. Remove from the heat and season with the salt and black pepper.

5. Fill the shells with the sautéed vegetable mixture. Place them on a rimmed baking sheet and top them with breadcrumbs. Bake for 15 minutes, until heated through. Remove from the oven.

6. Transfer the baked shells to a serving platter and serve hot.

Tart Cherry Pecan Crisp

Tart cherry pie is one of my favorite desserts, but making and rolling out the crust is time consuming, so this easy crisp is a good substitute. The Michigan tart cherry season is very short; sometimes they are at the Market for only two weeks. When that happens, I like to buy them in bulk, pit them, and freeze them in gallon-size freezer bags. For this recipe, I first soak the cherries in ice water for three hours in the refrigerator, which helps firm them up, making pitting easier. The versatile crumble topping can be used for any lightly sweetened fruit mixture, including peaches, pears, or a mixture of berries.
—Carol Mighton Haddix, customer

---

1 quart (4 cups) tart cherries, pitted
2 tablespoons granulated sugar
1 cup all-purpose flour
½ cup packed light brown sugar
½ teaspoon ground cinnamon

¼ teaspoon salt
6 tablespoons cold unsalted butter,
    cut into pieces
½ cup chopped pecans

Prep time: 40 minutes

Cook time: 35 minutes

Makes 6 servings

1. Preheat the oven to 400°F.

2. In a large bowl, combine the cherries and granulated sugar and mix well. Set aside.

3. In a medium bowl, combine the flour, brown sugar, cinnamon, and salt and mix well. Cut in the butter using a pastry blender (or do so quickly using your fingers) until small pea-sized chunks form. Stir in the pecans.

4. Place the cherry mixture in an 8- or 9-inch-square baking pan. Place the topping mixture on top of the cherries. Bake for 30 to 35 minutes, until the topping is browned and the filling is bubbling. Remove from the oven and let stand 20 minutes before serving.

5. Serve warm or at room temperature.

Perfect Peach Pie

When peaches are in season, I love to make this pie, which is one of my family's favorite desserts. To quickly peel the peaches, blanch them by cooking them for 1 minute in simmering water and then transferring them to an ice bath. Use a small paring knife to grab and slip off the skin. Before you make the pastry, place the butter and the food processor bowl and blade in the freezer to keep the butter from softening too much during the mixing process. It's possible to make a variation of this recipe using rhubarb bought during the springtime. Simply blanch it and store it in the freezer, and substitute 2 cups of rhubarb for 2 of the cups of peaches—but be sure to increase the amount of sugar to 1 cup. Peaches and rhubarb make a lovely combination. —**Corrine Kozlak, customer**

FOR THE PASTRY:
- 2½ cups all-purpose flour
- 2 tablespoons sugar
- ¼ teaspoon salt
- ½ cup shortening
- ½ cup very cold unsalted butter, cut into small cubes (freeze for 10 minutes before using)
- 6–7 tablespoons ice water, divided

FOR THE PIE:
- ½ cup sugar, plus more as needed
- 3 tablespoons quick-cooking tapioca
- 4 cups peeled, pitted, and sliced (about 6 whole) peaches
- 3 tablespoons orange juice or Grand Marnier
- 1 tablespoon unsalted butter, melted
- 1 egg, beaten
- 2 teaspoons water

Prep time: 30 minutes
Chill time: 30 minutes
Cook time: 55 minutes
Makes 6 to 8 servings

TO MAKE THE PASTRY:

1. In the bowl of a food processor, combine the flour, sugar, and salt. Pulse several times until combined. Add the shortening and pulse until just combined. Add the butter and pulse until the mixture looks like coarse meal.

2. Add 3 tablespoons of the ice water and pulse until combined. Continue adding the ice water, 1 tablespoon at a time, while pulsing just until dough holds together when pressed.

3. Divide the dough in half and transfer the halves to 2 sheets of plastic wrap. Using the heel of your hand, quickly work the dough together. Form each half into a disc. Wrap each disc in the plastic wrap and refrigerate for at least 30 minutes or up to 1 hour.

4. Lightly flour a pastry cloth or work surface. Roll out 1 disc of the dough into an 11-inch circle. Trim the edges evenly to form a 10-inch circle. Transfer the pastry to a 9-inch pie pan, pressing down on the bottom and sides to fit. Trim the pastry to ½ inch beyond the edge of the pie pan.

TO MAKE THE PIE:

1. Preheat the oven to 375°F.

2. In a large bowl, combine the sugar and tapioca and mix well. Add the peaches, orange juice, and butter and mix well. Spoon the mixture into the prepared pie shell.

3. On the pastry cloth, roll out the remaining disc of dough into an 11-inch circle. Place the circle of dough over the pie filling and tuck the edges under the bottom crust, or cut the rolled dough into ½-inch to ¾-inch strips and weave them together atop the pie filling to form a lattice topping over the pie. Flute the edges, and if using a full crust on top of the pie, cut several slits in the top crust to vent.

4. In a small bowl, beat the egg with the water. Brush the egg wash lightly over the top pie crust and discard the remaining egg wash. Sprinkle additional sugar evenly over the pie.

5. Place the pie on a rimmed baking sheet and bake for 30 minutes. After that time, check to see if the edges of the crust are browning too quickly; if so, tent the pie with foil.

6. Continue baking for 20 to 25 minutes, until the crust is golden brown and the filling is bubbly. Remove from the oven, transfer to a wire cooling rack, and let cool for at least 30 minutes. Serve warm or at room temperature.

Apricot Cobbler with Beurre Noisette and Crunchy Spiced Sugar

I love this recipe because it comes together in minutes—browning butter, hand mixing a quick batter, and simmering the apricots. Apricots are one of my favorite stone fruits, and a stroll through the Market without purchasing these luscious beauties is impossible! Tart, sweet, and a wonderful addition to this delicious fruit cobbler, they impart a caramelized, nutty flavor when baked with brown butter. Topped with crunchy demerara sugar and perfumed with a hint of cardamom and freshly grated nutmeg, this dessert is minimal work with maximum reward. Serve it warm or at room temperature with a scoop of vanilla ice cream.

—Malika Ameen, chef/owner, ByMDesserts

FOR THE FRUIT AND THE BEURRE NOISETTE:

1 pound apricots, cut into ½- to ¾-inch pieces

¼ to ⅓ cup organic cane sugar, depending on sweetness of fruit

1 teaspoon fresh lemon juice

⅛ teaspoon kosher salt

4 tablespoons (2 ounces) unsalted butter

FOR THE COBBLER TOPPING:

¾ cup all-purpose flour

½ cup organic cane sugar

1½ teaspoons baking powder

½ teaspoon kosher salt

½ teaspoon ground cinnamon

¾ cup buttermilk

½ teaspoon pure vanilla extract

⅓ cup fresh blueberries

FOR THE CRUNCHY SPICED SUGAR:

3 tablespoons demerara (turbinado) sugar

½ teaspoon ground cardamom

¼ teaspoon freshly grated nutmeg

Vanilla ice cream or crème Chantilly, for serving (optional)

Prep time: 30 minutes

Cook time: 1 hour 10 minutes

Makes 6 to 8 servings

TO MAKE THE FRUIT AND THE BEURRE NOISETTE:

1. Preheat the oven to 350°F.

2. In a medium saucepan over medium heat, combine the apricots, sugar, lemon juice, and salt. Bring just to a simmer. Remove from the heat and set aside to cool.

3. In a small saucepan over medium heat, melt the butter and cook for 2 minutes, until it begins to smell very nutty. Swirl the butter in the pan and continue to cook for 3 minutes, until the butter becomes golden and dark brown flecks start to appear. Remove from the heat and pour the browned butter into a 9-inch ceramic baking dish or glass pie plate. Set aside.

TO MAKE THE COBBLER TOPPING:

1. In a large bowl, whisk together the flour, sugar, baking powder, salt, and cinnamon. Add the buttermilk and vanilla and whisk just until the dry ingredients are moistened.

2. Using an ice cream scoop, place dollops of the Cobbler Topping batter over the brown butter, being careful not to mix it into the butter (some of the butter may seep through, which is okay). Scatter the apricots and their juices over the batter, still being sure not to mix them. Scatter the blueberries over the fruit.

3. Bake for 25 minutes.

TO MAKE THE CRUNCHY SPICED SUGAR AND THE FINISHED DISH:

1. While the cobbler is baking, in a medium bowl, combine the sugar, cardamom, and nutmeg and mix well.

2. Remove the cobbler from the oven after the first 25 minutes of baking time and sprinkle the Crunchy Spiced Sugar mainly over the cobbler topping. Bake for 25 to 30 minutes, until golden brown. Serve warm or at room temperature with the vanilla ice cream or crème Chantilly, if desired.

Summertime Berry Pie

Nothing says summer better than fresh blueberry pie. The key to this recipe is tossing the berries with the hot raspberry sauce. The berries stay firm, yet sweet and flavorful. A scoop of vanilla ice cream only makes it better! —**Carol Smoler, volunteer**

1 pint fresh raspberries
⅔ cup sugar
2 tablespoons cornstarch
¼ cup fresh lemon juice
3 pints fresh blueberries

1 (9-inch) pie crust, baked and cooled
Fresh mint leaves, for garnish
Shredded lemon peel, for garnish
Vanilla ice cream, for serving (optional)

Prep time: 30 minutes
Cook time: 10 minutes
Makes 8 servings

1. In a blender, purée the raspberries until smooth and press the mixture through a chinois or other fine mesh strainer to remove all seeds.

2. Transfer the raspberry purée to a medium saucepan over medium–high heat. Stir in the sugar and bring the mixture to a boil. Reduce the heat to low.

3. In a small bowl, combine the cornstarch and lemon juice and mix well. Add the cornstarch slurry to the saucepan. Cook, stirring constantly, for 2 to 3 minutes, until the mixture thickens. Remove from the heat.

4. Gently stir the blueberries into the warm sauce. Pour the sauce immediately into the prepared pie crust. Allow the pie to cool to room temperature. Serve garnished with the mint and lemon peel, and with the ice cream, if using.

Fall

When the air grows crisp as a fresh-picked apple, we know that fall has arrived. At the Market, grapes, pears, cider, squash, pumpkins, parsnips, peppers, and potatoes all compete for our attention, their colors reflecting the changing leaves and an earlier-setting sun.

By the end of October, farmers will harvest the last of their crops, putting their fields to bed until spring. Meanwhile, we'll relish the cool autumn air, sip warm soups, and savor hearty, comforting dishes.

Recipes

Farm Mint Pesto

Our mint pesto has become so popular at the Market that it has even begun to outsell our classic Rustic Basil Pesto. For this pesto, we use a pure strain of spearmint grown from seeds we acquired years ago from original mint plants grown on Richters Herbs in Canada. At Kinnikinnick Farm, we use mint pesto with everything from cold rice salads to pasta and grilled lamb, or we just keep it simple and serve it as a dip for raw vegetables, adding slightly more oil for a smoother consistency. —**Dave Cleverdon, farmer, Kinnikinnick Farm; Green City Market board member**

1 large clove garlic, peeled
2½ cups packed mint leaves, stems removed
½ cup packed fresh spinach or bietina greens
¼ cup grated aged Wisconsin Asiago cheese

¼ cup olive oil
¼ teaspoon coarse sea salt, plus more to taste
⅛ teaspoon freshly ground black pepper, plus more to taste

Prep time: 15 minutes

Makes ¾ cup pesto

1. Using a food processor with the motor running, drop the garlic through the feed tube and process until minced. Add the mint and spinach and pulse until finely chopped.

2. With the motor still running, slowly drizzle in the oil in a stream, emulsifying the pesto and processing it until it is thick and well combined. Stop the processor motor.

3. Add the cheese, salt, and black pepper and pulse just until blended. Season with additional salt and black pepper, if desired.

4. Transfer to a serving bowl and serve immediately, or store in an airtight container in the refrigerator for up to 5 days or in the freezer for up to 3 months.

Wisconsin Blue Cheese Dip

I am always looking for quick, delicious recipes that highlight Wisconsin cheese and pair well with our organic crackers available at the Market. Try our caramelized onion crackers with the dip for a savory flavor and our rhubarb graham crackers for a sweeter contrast.
—**Nancy Potter, vendor, Potter's Organic Artisan Crackers**

⅔ cup mascarpone cheese
⅓ cup crumbled blue or Gorgonzola cheese
¼ cup chopped toasted pecans

Honey, as needed, for drizzling
Organic crackers, any flavor, for serving

Prep time: 20 minutes
Makes 8 appetizer servings

1. In a small bowl, combine the mascarpone and blue cheeses and mix well.

2. Spread the cheese mixture into a shallow serving bowl. Top with the pecans and drizzle lightly with the honey. Refrigerate until ready to serve with the crackers.

Butternut Squash and Kale Soup

This hearty soup is great for warming up on a colder day. I like to pair it with crusty bread to soak up the deliciously spiced broth. The soup is even better a day or two after it's made, when the flavors have fully blended. Freeze it in batches for up to 3 months.
—**Hannah Altshuler, customer**

2 tablespoons olive oil

1 large onion, chopped

1 large butternut squash, peeled, cubed (about 4 cups)

5 carrots, thinly sliced or chopped

4 cloves garlic, minced

1 tablespoon ground cumin

½ to 1 teaspoon ground cinnamon, as desired

5 cups vegetable broth or water

1 bunch kale, tough stems discarded, leaves coarsely chopped

Salt, to taste

Freshly ground black pepper, to taste

Prep time: 20 minutes

Cook time: 35 minutes

Makes 6 servings (about 9 cups)

1. In a large saucepan over medium heat, warm the oil. Add the onion and sauté for 5 minutes, until translucent. Add the squash, carrots, garlic, cumin, and cinnamon to the saucepan and sauté for 5 minutes.

2. Raise the heat to high and stir in the broth. Bring to a boil. Reduce the heat to medium, cover, and simmer for 25 minutes, until the vegetables are very tender.

3. Stir in the kale and cook for 3 minutes. Remove from the heat and season with the salt and black pepper.

4. Transfer to 6 small serving bowls and serve hot.

Sausage Potato Soup

My husband's assistant, LeeAnn Coffelt, created this recipe, which makes a bracing meal on a crisp fall day. Depending on my mood, I regulate the degree of "fire" in the dish by choosing mild or hot sausage, and I add more or less spinach according to my whim and what I have on hand. The recipe is almost foolproof and my family loves it. —**Virginia Gerst, Green City Market board member**

1 pound mild or hot Italian sausage, in links or bulk

1 small onion, chopped

2 teaspoons minced garlic

8 cups chicken stock or broth

2 teaspoons dried oregano

2 teaspoons caraway seed

2 teaspoons ground cumin

1 teaspoon crushed red pepper flakes (optional)

4 medium potatoes (about 1½ pounds), peeled and cubed into small pieces

2 to 3 cups fresh spinach, coarsely chopped, tough stems removed

½ cup half and half

Prep time: 40 minutes

Cook time: 30 minutes

Makes 6 to 8 servings

1. If the sausage has casings, remove them. Crumble the sausage into a large saucepan over medium heat. Cook, stirring frequently, for 5 minutes, until the sausage is lightly browned. Pour off the drippings.

2. Add the onion and garlic to the saucepan and sauté for 5 minutes.

3. Increase the heat to high and add the stock, oregano, caraway seed, cumin, and red pepper flakes, if using, to the saucepan. Bring to a boil. Stir in the potatoes.

4. Reduce the heat to medium. Cover and simmer for 10 minutes, until the potatoes are tender.

5. Stir in the spinach and half and half and simmer for 3 to 4 minutes, until heated through. Remove from the heat.

6. Transfer to serving bowls and serve hot.

Parsnip Soup with Confit Mushrooms and Spiced Walnuts

This soup was inspired by my deep love for root vegetables, especially parsnips and celeriac. Earthy mushrooms slowly cooked in fat are rich and define the soup's texture and complexity, while the walnuts' natural bitterness contrasts with the sweetness of the parsnips. Thanks to Green City Market, I can see our farmer partners on a weekly basis, along with many of our regular customers and fellow chefs. I'm always inspired by seeing all of the available produce in the open-air setting. It's a beautiful way to shop. —**Michael Kornick, chef/owner, MK, DMK Burger, Fish Bar, Ada Street, County Barbeque, and DMK Burger & Fish**

FOR THE SOUP:

2 tablespoons organic unsalted butter
2 medium yellow onions, diced
2 pounds parsnips, peeled, diced
4 cups water or vegetable stock
2 tablespoons honey
Salt, to taste
Freshly ground black pepper, to taste
1 teaspoon ground cumin

FOR THE MUSHROOMS:

1 pound assorted mushrooms, as desired
Salt
2 cups sunflower oil or grape seed oil

1 large shallot, chopped
3 sprigs thyme
3 sprigs rosemary
3 bay leaves

FOR THE SPICED WALNUTS:

1 cup walnut halves or black walnut halves, toasted if desired
⅓ cup sugar
2 tablespoons organic unsalted butter
½ teaspoon ground cinnamon
⅛ teaspoon cayenne pepper

FOR THE FINISHED SOUP:

Chopped fresh chives, for garnish

Prep time: 15 minutes
Cook time: 1 hour
Makes 6 servings

TO MAKE THE SOUP:

1. In a large saucepan over medium heat, melt the butter. Add the onions. Reduce the heat to low, cover, and cook for 10 minutes, stirring occasionally.

2. Add the parsnips to the saucepan and stir well to combine. Cover and cook for 15 minutes, stirring occasionally, until the parsnips are tender.

Continued

3. Add the water and honey to the saucepan and stir well to combine. Simmer, covered, for 45 minutes, stirring occasionally. Remove from the heat.

4. Transfer the soup to a blender or food processor in batches and purée it. For a silkier texture, strain the soup through a chinois or other fine strainer (not necessary if you enjoy a heartier soup). Season with the salt and black pepper. Stir in the cumin. Set aside.

TO MAKE THE MUSHROOMS:

1. If the mushrooms are large, halve or quarter them. Place them in a large bowl, add the salt, and toss well.

2. In a 2-quart saucepan over low heat, warm the oil to 150°F.

3. Make a *bouquet garni* by placing the shallot, thyme, rosemary, and bay leaves in a piece of cheesecloth, forming a pouch, and tying a long piece of kitchen twine to close the pouch. Add the *bouquet garni* to the saucepan.

4. Add the mushrooms to the saucepan. Stir well to combine, then cover, and cook, stirring occasionally, for 1 hour, until the mushrooms are very tender. Be sure not to let the oil get too hot; the mushrooms should poach rather than fry. Remove from the heat.

5. Drain the mushrooms well and reserve the oil for later use (for example, in a salad dressing or to sauté spinach for a wilted salad). Discard the *bouquet garni*. Place the mushrooms on a plate lined with paper towels and set aside.

TO MAKE THE SPICED WALNUTS:

1. Coarsely chop the walnuts and set aside.

2. In an 8-inch skillet over medium heat, melt the butter. Add the sugar, cinnamon, and cayenne pepper and stir to combine.

3. When the butter begins to sizzle, add the walnuts. Stir constantly while cooking for 3 to 5 minutes, until the walnuts are coated with the butter mixture. Remove from the heat. Pour the walnuts onto a sheet of parchment paper or foil and let cool.

TO MAKE THE FINISHED SOUP:

1. Return the soup to the large saucepan it was prepared in and warm it up over medium heat. Remove from the heat.

2. Ladle the soup into shallow bowls. Top with the mushrooms and walnuts. Garnish with the chives and serve hot.

Apple, Carrot, and Beet Slaw

This is a wonderful way to use the best of the fall produce. The colorful slaw is so sweet and juicy on its own that it needs no dressing. It's the perfect dish to take to a potluck.
—**Lynn Gerstein, customer**

---

1 pound beets (about 4 medium, may be a mix of red and golden)
1 bunch carrots (about 1 pound), scrubbed or peeled

2 tart apples, cored, with skin on

Prep time: 30 minutes
Cook time: 50 minutes
Makes 16 ½-cup servings

1. Preheat the oven to 400°F. Tightly wrap each of the beets in foil.

2. Bake the beets for 40 to 50 minutes, until tender when pierced with a knife. Remove from the oven and set aside to cool.

3. Slice the carrots and apples into pieces that will fit into the feed tube of a food processor fitted with the shredding blade. Using the food processor, shred the carrots and apples and transfer them to a large serving bowl.

4. Peel or scrub the cooled beets. Cut them into pieces small enough to fit through the food processor's feed tube and shred them as well. Add the shredded beets to the bowl and toss well.

5. Serve immediately or cover and store in the refrigerator for up to 3 days.

Brussels Sprout, Apple, and Blue Cheese Salad

A few years ago, I found a few too many Brussels sprouts in my bag, along with red onion, red apples, and blue cheese, after a morning of shopping at the Market. One night, after a few glasses of wine, this recipe came to me. It is now my go-to salad whenever I see fresh Brussels sprouts for sale. The salad can be served warm, at room temperature, or chilled.
—**Laura Lamar, customer**

3 tablespoons olive oil

¾ pound Brussels sprouts, trimmed and quartered

1 small red apple, diced

¼ cup sliced or chopped red onion

¼ cup crumbled blue cheese

¼ cup chopped pecans or walnuts, toasted

4 teaspoons balsamic glaze or balsamic vinaigrette

Freshly ground black pepper (optional)

Prep time: 20 minutes

Cook time: 10 minutes

Makes 4 side-dish servings

1. In a 10-inch skillet over medium heat, warm the oil. Add the Brussels sprouts and sauté for 5 to 6 minutes, until almost tender.

2. Add the apple and onion to the skillet and sauté for 3 minutes. Remove from the heat.

3. Transfer the Brussels sprouts mixture to 4 serving plates and top with the blue cheese and pecans. Drizzle 1 teaspoon of the balsamic glaze over each salad. Season with the black pepper, if desired, and serve.

Whole-Wheat Fettuccine with Fall Harvest Vegetables

This flavorful recipe speaks of the autumn harvest, when butternut squash is at its best. Whole-wheat pasta is a healthful, hearty option that's great for fall. The recipe is also a fine example of the "Mediterranean diet" cuisine that's becoming increasingly popular.
—**Noe Sanchez, executive chef, Convito Café and Market**

½ cup extra virgin olive oil,
   plus more for serving
4 cups peeled, seeded, and cubed
   (½-inch pieces) butternut squash
¼ teaspoon salt, plus more to taste
4 cups chopped leeks (white and
   light green parts)

4 cups packed baby spinach, coarsely chopped
Freshly ground black pepper, to taste
2 (8-ounce) packages fresh whole-wheat
   fettuccine
5 ounces creamy goat cheese

Prep time: 30 minutes

Cook time: 10 minutes

Makes 6 servings

1. In a large, deep sauté pan over high heat, warm the oil. Add the squash and the ¼ teaspoon salt and sauté for 5 minutes, until golden brown. Add the leeks and sauté for 2 minutes. Add the spinach to the skillet and cook for 1 minute, tossing constantly, until the spinach is just wilted. Remove from the heat and season with the salt and black pepper.

2. Prepare the fettuccine according to the package directions. Remove from the heat.

3. Drain the pasta and transfer it to 6 shallow bowls. Top with the squash mixture. Drizzle with additional oil and spoon dots of the goat cheese over each serving. Serve warm.

Pork Chops with Apple Chutney

This speedy weeknight dinner tastes fresh even if the pork chops are pulled out of the freezer. It feels good to put such a pretty, delicious dish on the table so quickly after getting home from work. —**Pam Lamaster-Millett, customer**

1 teaspoon coconut oil or olive oil
2 bone-in pork chops
Salt, to taste
Freshly ground black pepper, to taste
1 tablespoon unsalted butter
1 red apple, unpeeled, chopped

1 to 2 fresh habanero or serrano chile peppers, seeded, minced
1 teaspoon chopped fresh mint leaves or favorite fresh herb
2 teaspoons apple jelly

Prep time: 15 minutes

Cook time: 12 minutes

Makes 2 to 4 servings, depending on size of pork chops

1. Spread the oil over the pork chops (thawed if using frozen) and season with the salt and black pepper. Warm a nonstick skillet or grill pan over medium heat or preheat a grill to medium (300°F to 350°F).

2. Place the chops in the skillet or on the grill and cook for 3 to 6 minutes per side, depending on the thickness of chops. Remove from the heat or grill and transfer to a platter tented with foil.

3. In a small skillet over medium heat, melt the butter. Add the apple and peppers and sauté for 5 minutes, until tender. Stir in the mint and jelly and sauté for 1 minute. Remove from the heat.

4. Serve the chutney over the warm pork chops.

Papa's Sausage and Peppers

My family loves this hearty main dish. After watching the movie Dinner Rush, *in which the chef prepares his father's favorite dish, sausage and peppers, I decided to make my own version. I buy dried white beans from Nichols Farm & Orchard, cook them in lots of water until tender, and then store them in the refrigerator. The sausage comes from Jake's Country Meats and pairs well with the colorful bell peppers that brighten the Market in early fall. A mixed green salad with fresh herbs and balsamic dressing is the perfect light accompaniment to this dish.* —**Karen Levin, volunteer**

---

1 tablespoon olive oil
1 pound hot or sweet Italian sausage links
1 medium onion, cut into 1-inch chunks
3 small bell peppers, preferably a mix of
    colors, cut into 1-inch chunks (3 cups)

½ teaspoon salt
¼ teaspoon freshly ground black pepper
½ cup dry red wine
2 cups cooked white beans
2 tablespoons chopped fresh rosemary

Prep time: 20 minutes

Cook time: 50 minutes

Makes 4 servings

1. Preheat the oven to 350°F.

2. In a large, deep, ovenproof skillet over medium heat, warm the oil. Add the sausage links and cook for 3 minutes per side, until just lightly browned.

3. Add the onion to the skillet and cook for 1 minute. Add the peppers and season with the salt and black pepper. Add the wine to skillet and remove it from the heat. Transfer the skillet to the oven.

4. Bake for 30 to 35 minutes, until the sausage is no longer pink in the center and the vegetables are tender. Remove from the oven and stir in the cooked beans. Return to the oven and bake for 5 minutes, until the beans have heated. Remove from the oven.

5. Top with the rosemary and serve hot in the skillet.

French-Roasted Chicken Thighs

PICTURED ON PAGE 120

This is a succulent roasted chicken dish with classic flavors and a traditional preparation. I love to make it because everyone enjoys it so much! I prepared it several years ago for a birthday party in the south of France using the famous Bresse chicken breed from the Rhône-Alpes region and herbes de Provence, both from the local market. Ever since then I use only fresh Green City Market chickens and local herbs; it makes all the difference. With good bread and wine, it is even more delicious. —**Elizabeth Crawford, customer**

1 medium onion, coarsely chopped

1 head garlic, cloves separated, unpeeled

2 pounds bone-in chicken thighs, excess fat trimmed (about 8 thighs)

8 medium red potatoes (about 1½ pounds)

2 tablespoons Dijon mustard

1 tablespoon herbes de Provence or 1 teaspoon each dried rosemary, thyme and marjoram

1 teaspoon sea salt

1 teaspoon freshly ground black pepper

½ cup chicken broth or stock

½ cup dry white wine

Prep time: 20 minutes

Cook time: 55 minutes

Makes 4 servings

1. Preheat the oven to 350°F.

2. In a 13 × 9-inch baking dish, arrange the onion and garlic cloves. Arrange the chicken, skin side up, on top of the onion mixture. Place the potatoes around the chicken.

3. Spread the mustard evenly over the chicken. Sprinkle the herbes de Provence, salt, and black pepper over the chicken. Pour the broth and wine over the chicken and cover the dish tightly with foil.

4. Bake for 30 minutes. Remove the foil and raise the oven temperature to 400°F. Continue baking for 20 to 25 minutes, basting the chicken with the juices from the dish twice, until the chicken is golden brown and the internal temperature reaches 160°F. Remove from the oven.

5. Transfer the chicken and potatoes to a serving platter and tent with foil to keep them warm.

6. Into a medium saucepan over high heat, pour the juices from the baking dish through a strainer. Discard the solids from the strainer. Bring the juices to a boil.

7. Reduce the heat to medium and simmer for 6 to 8 minutes, until the sauce has reduced to ¾ cup. Remove from the heat.

8. Transfer the sauce to a serving pitcher and serve separately with the warm chicken and potatoes.

French-Roasted Chicken Thighs
Recipe on page 118

Roast Turkey with Spice Rub and Beer Gravy
Recipe on page 122

Roast Turkey with Spice Rub and Beer Gravy

PICTURED ON PAGE 121

Just in time for Thanksgiving, here's a new twist on the traditional roast turkey. The secret to making a great turkey is a two-step cooking process. For most of a turkey's cooking time, it should be covered in the oven so it stays moist. Then, at the end, it should be uncovered. The oven temperature is raised, the skin is basted, and eventually the skin becomes browned. I am not a fan of stuffing turkey, as the meat is usually overcooked by the time the stuffing is done.
—**Chris Koetke, vice president, Kendall College, School of Culinary Arts**

⅔ cup light brown sugar

2½ tablespoons paprika

1½ tablespoons freshly ground black pepper, plus more to taste

2½ teaspoons salt, plus more to taste

1½ teaspoons garlic powder

1¼ teaspoons ground thyme

1 teaspoon ground cumin

1 (10-pound) fresh or thawed turkey

1 (12-ounce) bottle ale or beer

½ pound cipollini and/or small purple onions

1 stalk celery, cut into thick slices

1 large carrot, cut into thick slices

1 bay leaf

¼ cup unsalted butter, melted

¼ cup Dijon mustard

¼ cup all-purpose flour mixed with ½ cup cold water

Savory sprigs (optional)

Prep time: 20 minutes

Cook time: 3 to 3½ hours

Serves: 8 to 10

1. Preheat the oven to 350°F.

2. In a small bowl, combine the brown sugar, paprika, black pepper, salt, garlic powder, thyme, and cumin. Stir well.

3. Rinse and thoroughly dry the turkey inside and out. Place the turkey on a rack set inside a roasting pan. Rub the spice mixture all over the turkey, including inside its cavity.

4. Pour the ale into the bottom of the roasting pan. Arrange the onions, celery, and carrot in the ale around the turkey. Add enough water so that there are about 1½ inches of liquid in the bottom of the roasting pan. Cover the turkey loosely with aluminum foil.

5. Roast the turkey for 2 hours. Check the temperature of the turkey breast at the deepest part (taking care not to touch the bone) with an instant-read thermometer. Once the internal temperature reaches 130°F, increase the oven temperature to 425°F and brush the turkey with some of the melted butter.

6. Continue roasting and basting the turkey with butter every 15 minutes until the turkey's internal temperature reaches 165°F. At this point, the turkey's skin should be roasted to a rich brown color. Remove from the oven, transfer the turkey to a carving board, and cover with foil. Let stand for at least 25 minutes before carving.

7. Pour the juices from the roasting pan through a strainer into a small saucepan. Discard the solids from the strainer and discard the vegetables from the pan. Skim and discard the fat from the juices. Whisk in the mustard and then the flour mixture until smooth. Bring to a boil.

8. Reduce the heat to medium and simmer for 5 minutes (for thicker gravy, simmer longer until it reaches the desired consistency). Taste the gravy and season with the salt and black pepper if needed. Remove from the heat.

9. Carve the turkey. Transfer the gravy to a serving pitcher and serve separately with the warm turkey garnished with the savory sprigs (if using).

Grilled Coulotte Steak

The coulotte is the cap of the top butt, or sirloin, steak. Just as the outer "cap" of a rib eye is more tender than the eye, the coulotte is more tender than the sirloin steak, and just as lean and full of flavor. Our coulottes range from 1 to 2 pounds, with 1¼ pounds being the most common size. They make a great choice for families and for those individuals with heartier appetites. —**Pat Sondgeroth, farmer, Heartland Meats**

1 tablespoon olive oil
1 tablespoon red wine
1 tablespoon balsamic glaze
2 teaspoons chopped fresh parsley

1 to 2 teaspoons chopped fresh rosemary
½ teaspoon sea salt
½ teaspoon freshly ground black pepper
1 (1¼-pound) coulotte steak

Prep time: 10 minutes
Cook time: 14 to 20 minutes
Resting time: 10 to 15 minutes
Makes 4 to 5 servings

1. In a small bowl, combine all the ingredients except the steak and mix well. Brush half of the mixture over both sides of the steak and let stand at room temperature for 15 to 30 minutes.

2. Preheat the grill to medium (300°F to 350°F).

3. Place the steak on the grill, cover the grill, and cook for 8 minutes. Brush half of the remaining glaze on the top side of the steak and then turn it over and brush the remainder of the glaze on the other side. Cover the grill and cook for 8 to 10 minutes, until the internal temperature of the steak reaches 120°F for medium rare. Remove from the grill and transfer the steak to a carving board tented with foil. Let stand for 10 to 15 minutes before carving.

4. Slice the steak thinly across the grain and serve warm.

🥄 COOK'S NOTE

This steak may also be oven roasted. To oven roast, brush all of the glaze over both sides of the steak and roast in a 425°F oven for 15 to 20 minutes, until the internal temperature reaches 120°F. Continue the recipe as directed.

Pumpkin–Parmesan Gnocchi with Turkey, Sage, Pears, and Pecans

This dish really captures so much of what makes autumn in the Midwest delicious. Harvested and cured fall pumpkins with delicious Michigan pears, sage, and local turkey (or leftovers from a Thanksgiving-style feast) make this an easy plan-ahead option for the beautiful crisp, clear nights we enjoy here. —**Bruce Sherman, chef/owner, North Pond; Green City Market board member**

FOR THE APPLE CIDER SYRUP:

½ cup fresh pressed, unfiltered apple cider

½ cup apple cider vinegar

1 tablespoon unsalted butter, chilled

FOR THE GNOCCHI:

1 cup puréed, roasted sugar pumpkin flesh*

1 cup roasted russet potato flesh*

1 large egg, beaten

¾ cup finely grated Parmesan cheese, plus shaved for garnish

½ teaspoon salt

½ teaspoon ground white pepper

⅛ teaspoon grated nutmeg

¾ cup all-purpose flour, plus more for dusting

FOR THE BROWNED BUTTER TOPPING:

½ cup organic unsalted butter

18 to 20 fresh sage leaves, finely chopped

¾ cup diced (½ inch) cooked turkey

¾ cup chopped pecans, toasted

1 ripe D'Anjou or Bosc pear, peeled and diced (about ¾ cup)

Salt, to taste

Freshly ground black pepper, to taste

FOR FINISHING THE DISH:

1–2 tablespoons chopped fresh parsley (optional), for garnish

Prep time: 1 hour

Cook time: 1 hour

Makes 4 to 6 servings

TO MAKE THE APPLE CIDER SYRUP:

1. In a small, nonreactive saucepan over medium heat, bring the cider and cider vinegar to a boil.

2. Reduce the heat to medium and simmer for 5 to 8 minutes, until the mixture has reduced to 3 tablespoons. (The liquid will have a syrup-like consistency.) Watch closely toward the end of the cooking time to prevent burning. Remove from the heat, whisk in the butter, and set aside.

Continued

TO MAKE THE GNOCCHI:

1. In a large bowl, combine the cooled pumpkin and potato. Add the egg, cheese, salt, white pepper, and nutmeg and mix well. Stir in the ¾ cup of flour until the mixture just holds together; do not over mix.

2. On a well-floured countertop or work surface, roll a baseball-sized amount of the dough forward and backward with the palms of both hands, gradually applying pressure to the center and outward in either direction. This should force the mixture into a long sausage-like shape. Continue rolling until it is about ¾ inch in diameter.

3. Repeat with the remaining dough, forming 1 or 2 more sausage-like shapes.

4. Cut the shapes into ½-inch pieces along the entire length of each tube. With a well-floured thumb or fork, carefully make an indentation into each piece.

5. Transfer the gnocchi to a well-floured baking sheet and refrigerate for at least 10 minutes or freeze for later use.

6. Bring a large saucepan of salted water over medium–high heat to a boil.

TO MAKE THE BROWNED BUTTER TOPPING:

1. In a large skillet over medium–low heat, warm the butter, stirring occasionally, until it sizzles. After 5 minutes, all the butter should be melted and browned and the sizzling should stop. Add the sage to the skillet, stirring once. Remove from the heat if the butter seems close to burning; otherwise, continue cooking over medium-low heat.

2. Add the turkey, pecans, and pear to the skillet and stir to coat. Cook for 1 minute, until warmed through. Remove from the heat, if necessary, and season with the salt and black pepper. Set aside.

* To roast and purée the pumpkin and potatoes: Slice the pumpkin in half and scoop out the seeds and stringy flesh. Brush with olive oil and bake in a 375°F oven with unpeeled russet potatoes (pierced) for 1 hour, until tender. Remove from the oven. Allow to cool to room temperature and then scoop out the pumpkin and potato flesh. Mash well.

TO FINISH THE DISH:

1. Carefully slide the gnocchi into the boiling water. Cook for 3 to 4 minutes, until the gnocchi begin to float. As each piece begins to float, scoop it out using a slotted spoon and place it in a large bowl.

2. After all the gnocchi have been cooked, remove the saucepan from the heat. Toss the gnocchi with the oil and divide them evenly into 4 to 6 serving bowls. Top with the Browned Butter Topping, garnish with the parsley (if using) and Parmesan cheese, and drizzle with the Apple Cider Syrup. Serve immediately.

New-World Cassoulet with Chilies and Turkey

Ever since I first tasted it, I've loved cassoulet. It's just a few simple ingredients from the larder like beans (mine were from Market vendor Three Sisters Garden), preserved meats, and a couple of storage vegetables made magical with slow cooking and a little patience. Finding beautiful local ingredients for all the important elements made my first months of building The Honest Meal Project—a yearlong commitment to eating only locally sourced foods—that much richer. Smoked turkey is a delicious stand-in for the classic confit, and local dried chilies stoke the internal furnace. The Honest Meal Project crafts locally sourced soups, salads, and purées for Green City Market's customers. —**Dana Cox Lipe, vendor, The Honest Meal Project**

FOR THE CASSOULET:

1 pound dried black turtle beans

2 tablespoons olive oil

2 cups diced onions

1 cup diced carrots

1 cup diced celery

6 tablespoons (about 12 cloves) minced garlic

2 teaspoons dried oregano

1 teaspoon dried thyme

2 bay leaves

3 dried chilies, such as ancho or guajillo, seeds and stems removed

1 cup dry white wine

1–2 cups chicken stock or water, divided

1 smoked turkey drumstick

½ pound slab or thickly sliced bacon

1 teaspoon cumin seed

½ pound turkey sausage

2 cups bottled whole tomatoes in juice, undrained

Salt, to taste

Freshly ground black pepper, to taste

FOR THE GARLIC BREADCRUMBS:

1 small baguette bread (6 to 7 inches long)

1 large clove garlic, peeled

⅛ teaspoon salt

⅛ teaspoon freshly ground black pepper

Soaking time for beans: overnight

Prep time: 50 minutes

Cook time: 2 hours 35 minutes

Makes 6 to 8 servings

TO MAKE THE CASSOULET:

1. Sort, rinse, and soak the beans in at least 8 cups of water overnight in a container large enough to allow them to double in size. Check frequently to ensure that the beans remain covered with water at all times.

2. In an 8-quart stockpot over medium-high heat, warm the oil. Add the onions, carrots, and celery and sauté for 5 minutes, until they start to brown.

3. Add the garlic, thyme, oregano, bay leaves, and chilies to the stockpot and continue cooking for 5 minutes, until the vegetables have softened. Deglaze the stockpot with the wine, scraping up any browned bits from the bottom.

4. Cook for 6 to 8 minutes, until the liquid reduces in volume by at least half.

5. Drain the beans and add them, along with 1 cup of the chicken stock, to the stockpot. Stir to combine.

6. Raise the heat to high, submerge the turkey drumstick in the stockpot, and bring to a boil.

7. Reduce the heat to low, cover, and cook for 1½ to 2 hours, occasionally stirring the beans. Check frequently to ensure that the beans remain covered with liquid at all times; if not, add another cup of the chicken stock. Test the beans for tenderness at 1½ hours; if they are not tender, continue to cook, checking every 15 minutes for doneness. Remove from the heat, remove and discard the bay leaves, and keep covered.

8. Cut the slab bacon into ¼-inch cubes (for sliced bacon, cut crosswise into ¼-inch strips). Place the bacon in a cold sauté pan or skillet. Place the pan over medium heat and cook for 8 to 10 minutes, turning frequently, until the fat is rendered and the bacon is brown and fairly crisp. Remove from the heat.

9. Remove the bacon from the pan with a slotted spoon and place it on a plate lined with paper towels. Remove and reserve all except 1 tablespoon of the fat from the pan and set aside in a small bowl.

10. Return the sauté pan containing the 1 tablespoon of bacon fat to medium–low heat. Add the cumin seeds and toast for 1 minute.

11. Raise the heat to medium and add the sausage to the pan. Cook, breaking up into pieces with a wooden spoon, for 10 to 12 minutes, until browned. Add the tomatoes and their juice to the pan and bring to a gentle boil.

12. Reduce the heat to low and simmer for 12 to 14 minutes, until the sauce thickens slightly. Remove from the heat.

Continued

New-World Cassoulet with Chilies and Turkey (continued)

TO MAKE THE GARLIC BREADCRUMBS:

1. Cut the baguette into 1-inch chunks.

2. In the bowl of a food processor, combine the bread chunks, garlic, salt, and black pepper. Pulse until the crumbs reach the desired coarseness.

TO FINISH THE DISH:

1. Preheat the oven to 375°F.

2. Remove the chilies from the stockpot. Mince them and return them to the stockpot, or simply discard them if you prefer a milder dish.

3. Remove the turkey leg from the stockpot and set it aside until it is cool enough to handle. Once it is, pull or cut the meat from the bone. Discard the skin, tendons, and bone (pay careful attention to removing the many small, flexible bones) and cut the meat into bite-sized chunks. Return the chunks of meat to the stockpot and stir well.

4. Add the tomato–sausage mixture and bacon to the stockpot and stir well. Season with the salt and black pepper.

5. Transfer the cassoulet to a shallow casserole dish or spoon 1½ cups of the cassoulet into each of 6 to 8 small casserole dishes. Top with the breadcrumbs and drizzle with the reserved bacon fat.

6. Bake, uncovered, for 30 to 35 minutes, until the cassoulet is heated through and the breadcrumbs are golden brown. Remove from the oven and serve hot.

Roasted Harvest Vegetables

I adapted this recipe from an old Chicago Tribune *clipping after shopping at Green City Market one day. It was a big hit with my friends around the fall holidays. I took it to a party, and the hostess invited another friend over the next day to enjoy the leftovers. They both came to my gym class raving about how delicious the dish was! It's also great for those looking to boost their vegetable intake.* —**Sheri Schneider, customer**

1 large sweet onion, cut into chunks

12 ounces whole cremini mushrooms, stems trimmed

1 pound turnips, peeled and cut into chunks

1 large rutabaga (12 ounces), peeled and cut into chunks

1 large red bell pepper, cut into chunks

12 ounces small potatoes, scrubbed and cut into chunks

8 ounces butternut squash, peeled, cut into 1-inch chunks

8 ounces medium-sized Brussels sprouts, trimmed and halved

⅓ cup olive oil

1½ teaspoons salt

¾ teaspoon freshly ground black pepper

¼ cup chopped fresh thyme leaves

2 tablespoons chopped fresh rosemary leaves

Prep time: 30 minutes

Cook time: 35 minutes

Makes 8 to 10 servings

1. Preheat the oven to 400°F.

2. In a very large bowl, combine all the ingredients, except the thyme and rosemary, and toss well.

3. Arrange the vegetables in a single layer in a large, heavy rimmed baking sheet or roasting pan.

4. Bake for 20 minutes. Remove from the oven and toss the vegetables. Return to the oven and continue baking for 15 minutes, until vegetables are tender and browned. Remove from the oven.

5. Transfer the vegetables to a large serving bowl. Add the thyme and rosemary and toss well. Serve hot.

Crispy Green Tomatoes with Arugula Pesto

A Chicago twist on a soul-food favorite, this recipe is my healthful version of a beloved family classic. I must have shared the idea for this recipe with dozens of customers at the Market, usually with three or four other shoppers eavesdropping on our conversation. Green tomatoes are available into the fall, and I'm happy to share the official recipe details here.
—**Erika Allen, farmer, Growing Power, Inc.**

FOR THE ARUGULA PESTO:

2 cloves garlic, peeled

2 cups (2 ounces) packed arugula leaves

2 tablespoons chopped fresh thyme or ¼ cup packed basil leaves

2 tablespoons extra virgin olive oil

¼ cup grated hard cheese, such as aged goat cheese (optional)

Kosher salt, to taste

Freshly ground black pepper, to taste

FOR THE CRISPY GREEN TOMATOES:

3 large green tomatoes (about 1½ pounds)

1 cup panko breadcrumbs*

¼ cup cornmeal

¼ cup all-purpose flour

1 teaspoon kosher salt

½ teaspoon freshly ground black pepper

Pinch of crushed red pepper flakes (optional)

1 large egg

¼ cup milk, soy milk, or almond milk

4 tablespoons extra virgin olive oil, divided

Kosher salt, for sprinkling (optional)

1 lemon, cut into 6 wedges, for serving

Prep time: 25 minutes

Cook time: 18 minutes

Makes 6 servings

TO MAKE THE ARUGULA PESTO:

1. Using a food processor with the motor running, drop the garlic through the feed tube and process until finely chopped. Stop the processor motor. Add the arugula and thyme and pulse until finely chopped.

2. With the motor running, slowly drizzle in the oil in a stream, emulsifying the pesto and processing it until it is thick and well combined. Stop the processor motor.

3. Add the cheese (if using) and pulse just until blended. Season with additional salt and black pepper. Set aside.

Continued

Crispy Green Tomatoes with Arugula Pesto (continued)

TO MAKE THE CRISPY GREEN TOMATOES:

1. Preheat the oven to 425°F.

2. Cut each tomato horizontally into ⅓-inch slices (4 to 5 slices per tomato).

3. In a shallow plate or pie dish, combine the breadcrumbs, cornmeal, flour, salt, and black pepper. Stir in the red pepper flakes, if using.

4. In another shallow plate or pie dish, beat the egg. Add the milk and 1 tablespoon of the oil and stir well.

5. Pour the remaining 3 tablespoons of oil into a 15 × 10-inch rimmed baking sheet. Tilt the sheet to ensure that it is evenly coated.

6. Dip 1 tomato slice in the egg mixture and then dredge it in the crumb mixture, patting to coat. Place the slice on the prepared baking sheet. Repeat until all the slices are on the baking sheet in a single layer.

7. Bake for 8 to 10 minutes, until the tomato slices are browned on the bottom. Remove from the oven, turn the slices over, and continue to bake for 6 to 8 minutes, until they are browned on the bottom. Remove from the oven.

8. Serve immediately, sprinkled with the salt (if using), and alongside the Arugula Pesto and lemon wedges.

* You can also make fresh breadcrumbs from your favorite vendor's bread; simply toast the crumbs until lightly golden.

Elaine and Gil's Applesauce

As it often does on the farm, time can get away from us. Once when that happened, one of our newest varieties of apples got overripe. Not wanting anything to go to waste, Mick picked the bushel of Dandee Red apples anyway, insisting that they would make the best sauce. We gave them to one of our most loyal Market customers to try, and she returned to us one of the best jars of applesauce we've ever had. If Dandee Red apples are not available, choose the Lucky Jonathan variety for a similar texture and flavor. —**Abby Klug Schilling, farmer, Mick Klug Farm**

2½ pounds Dandee red apples
2½ cups water
½ cup sugar

1 tablespoon fresh lemon juice
Ground nutmeg or cinnamon, to taste

Prep time: 20 minutes
Cook time: 10 minutes
Makes 6 to 8 servings

1. If you do not have a food mill, peel the apples. If you do have a food mill, just quarter and core the apples.

2. In a large saucepan over high heat, place the apples and cover with water. Bring to a boil.

3. Reduce the heat to medium, cover, and simmer for 10 minutes, until the apples are nearly soft.

4. Add the sugar, lemon juice, and nutmeg to the saucepan and stir well. Remove from the heat.

5. Using either a food mill or a potato masher, mash the apples.

6. Transfer to a bowl and serve, or chill to serve cold.

Sweet Potato Gratin with Fennel, Leek, and Garlic Breadcrumbs

PICTURED ON PAGE 140

This is a savory way to serve sweet potatoes at Thanksgiving. The sweetness of the potatoes along with the saltiness of the white Cheddar and feta make it a perfectly balanced side dish.
—**Dominic Benigno, customer**

4 large sweet potatoes

1 large fennel bulb and fronds

3 tablespoons unsalted butter, melted, divided

1 tablespoon olive oil

2 leeks, white and pale green parts only, thinly sliced

2 teaspoons kosher salt, divided

½ teaspoon freshly ground black pepper, divided

2 (3-inch-thick) slices day old French baguette, crusts included

1 clove garlic, peeled

2 tablespoons chopped fresh parsley

2 cups shredded white Cheddar cheese

1 cup crumbled feta cheese

1½ cups heavy whipping cream

¼ teaspoon grated nutmeg

Dash of cayenne pepper

Prep time: 30 minutes

Cook time: 50 minutes

Serves 6 to 8 as a side dish

1. Preheat the oven to 350°F.

2. Prick the sweet potatoes with a fork and cook in the microwave on high for 7 to 8 minutes or until barely tender. (They will cook a bit more during the cooling.) When cool enough to handle, peel the sweet potatoes and cut into ¼-inch slices. Slice the fennel bulb in half and remove the hard core; slice the bulb into thin slices. Reserve the fennel fronds for salads or garnish, if desired.

3. In a large skillet over medium heat, combine 1 tablespoon of the butter with the oil. Add the fennel and leeks and cook, stirring occasionally, for 8 to 10 minutes, until tender. Stir in 1 teaspoon of the salt and ¼ teaspoon of the black pepper, remove from the heat, and set aside.

4. Using a food processor, combine the bread, garlic, and parsley. Pulse until the crumbs reach the desired coarseness. Add the remaining butter and pulse until combined. Set aside.

5. Grease or spray a 13 × 9-inch baking dish. Layer ½ the sweet potato slices in the bottom of the dish. Top with ½ the fennel and leek mixture followed by ½ the Cheddar and feta cheeses. Layer again with the remaining ingredients until all have been used.

6. In a small bowl, combine the cream, the remaining 1 teaspoon salt, the remaining ¼ teaspoon black pepper, the nutmeg, and the cayenne pepper and stir well to combine. Pour evenly over the contents of the baking dish and top with the breadcrumbs.

7. Bake for 45 to 50 minutes, until the dish is bubbly and the breadcrumbs are golden brown. Remove from the oven.

8. Serve hot.

Sweet Potato Gratin with Fennel, Leek and Garlic Breadcrumbs
Recipe on page 138

Market Apple Pie
Recipe on page 142

Market Apple Pie

PICTURED ON PAGE 141

This is my favorite apple pie recipe because it uses at least three different types of apples for a filling with a very complex flavor profile and slightly varied texture. The seasoning is subtle and used to enhance, not mask, the apples. From Honeycrisp to Jonagold to heirloom varieties, the type of apples used never seems to matter as long as I end up with three kinds.
—**Jill Van Cleave, customer**

FOR THE CRUST:

2 cups all-purpose flour

½ teaspoon salt

6 tablespoons (3 ounces) unsalted butter, cold, cut into pieces

6 tablespoons (3 ounces) rendered leaf lard or additional butter, cold and cut into pieces

⅓ cup ice water

FOR THE FILLING:

6 medium apples, 2 each of 3 different varieties, peeled, cored, and cut into ¼-inch slices

¼ cup sugar

¼ cup brown sugar

Grated zest of 1 small lemon

¼ teaspoon ground ginger

⅛ teaspoon ground nutmeg

2½ tablespoons all-purpose flour

1 tablespoon unsalted butter, cut into pieces

Milk or cream, for brushing

Coarse or granulated sugar, for sprinkling

Prep time: 25 minutes

Chill time: 1 hour

Cook time: 55 minutes

Makes 8 servings

TO MAKE THE CRUST:

1. In a medium bowl, combine the flour and salt. Cut in the butter and lard using a pastry blender (or 2 knives) until small pea-sized chunks form.

2. Add 3 tablespoons of the ice water and mix until combined. Adding 1 additional tablespoon at a time, add just enough of the ice water to form a dough.

3. Divide the dough into ⅔ and ⅓ portions and place the portions on 2 sheets of plastic wrap. Using the heel of your hand, quickly work the dough together. Form each portion into a disc. Wrap each disc in the plastic wrap and refrigerate for at least 1 hour.

TO MAKE THE FILLING:

1. In a large bowl, combine the apples, sugars, lemon zest, ginger, and nutmeg. Add flour and mix well. Set aside.

TO ASSEMBLE AND BAKE THE PIE:

1. Preheat the oven to 400°F.

2. Lightly flour a pastry cloth or work surface. Roll out the larger disc of the dough into a 12-inch circle that is about ⅛ inch thick. Fit the disc into a 9-inch pie pan that is 1½ inches deep, pressing down on the bottom and sides to fit, and trim the edges evenly.

3. Fill the pie dish with the apple mixture. Arrange the pieces of butter over the apples.

4. On the pastry cloth, roll out the remaining disc of dough into a 10-inch circle of similar thickness for the top crust. Place the circle of dough over the pie filling and tuck the edges under the bottom crust. Crimp the edges together to seal, trimming any excess dough.

5. If desired, roll out any leftover scrapes of dough and cut leaf shapes with a cookie cutter. Carve the leaves with a toothpick for decoration and place around the edges of the pie.

6. Brush the top crust lightly with the milk and sprinkle with the coarse sugar. Cut slits in the top crust dough to release steam while baking.

7. Place the pie on a rimmed baking sheet and bake for 55 minutes, until the crust is golden brown and the filling is bubbly. Remove from the oven and place on a wire rack until cooled.

8. Serve warm or at room temperature.

Holiday Honey Cake with Raspberries

When I was 21 and newly married, I left the East Coast for southern Illinois. Since this was long before anyone dreamed of keeping in touch via cell phones or the Internet, my mother and I exchanged weekly letters. Often on her own, or whenever I asked, she would include one of her tried-and-true recipes. This is one she learned from her mother who, as a 16-year-old bride in the 1880s, brought it along with her samovar and featherbed to Philadelphia from Kiev. My mother always made this cake for our family on Rosh Hashanah. I added the amaretto, raspberries, and local Market honey that enhance this delicious cake.
—**Marsha Goldsmith Van, volunteer**

4 eggs, separated
¾ cup honey
¾ cup sugar
2 cups all-purpose flour
1 teaspoon baking powder
½ teaspoon ground cinnamon
¼ teaspoon salt

⅛ teaspoon cloves
⅛ teaspoon nutmeg
⅓ cup slivered almonds, toasted (optional)
3 tablespoons amaretto liqueur or bourbon, divided
2 cups fresh raspberries
1 tablespoon confectioners' sugar

Prep time: 15 minutes
Cook time: 45 to 50 minutes
Makes 9 servings

1. Preheat the oven to 350°F. Grease an 8- or 9-inch-square baking pan.

2. In a large bowl, using either a hand or stand mixer, beat the egg whites on low speed for 4 to 6 minutes, until they are stiff but not dry.

3. In a separate bowl, beat the egg yolks until they are light and lemon colored. While beating continuously, add the honey and sugar.

4. In a medium bowl, combine the flour, baking powder, cinnamon, salt, cloves, and nutmeg. Gradually add the dry mixture to the egg yolk mixture (blend well but do not overbeat).

5. Add 2 tablespoons of the amaretto. Fold the egg whites into the mixture. Fold the almonds, if using, into the mixture.

6. Transfer the mixture to the prepared baking pan and bake for 45 to 50 minutes, until golden brown and a wooden pick inserted in the cake's center comes out clean. Remove from the oven and transfer the cake to a wire rack to cool completely.

7. Using a thin metal spatula, separate the cake from the pan and turn it out onto a cutting board. Cut the cake into 9 equal-sized squares and place each square on a separate serving plate.

8. In a small bowl, toss the raspberries with the remaining 1 tablespoon of amaretto. Spoon ¼ cup of the raspberry mixture over each serving.

9. Place the confectioners' sugar in a sifter or strainer and shake it over each serving. Serve immediately.

Winter

For many Midwesterners, that first bone-chilling day can stir a sense of dread, yet it also means we'll soon be enjoying the robust and warming foods that appear in winter.

For some farmers, this time of year marks a much-needed break, but many extend the season through greenhouses sprouting microgreens, hardy spinach and chard, and a variety of other fresh greens. Others bring to the market their foraged pecans, homemade pickles, herb-infused jams, and summertime sauces, adding interest to the slow-cooked roasts and simmering stews that warm and perfume our kitchens.

Recipes

Gravlax with Honey Mustard–Dill Sauce

Inspired by our honeymoon trip to Scandinavia, I have often made gravlax (salt-cured salmon) for parties over the years. It's easy to make ahead and, most important, it tastes delicious! Although far from Stockholm, Green City Market has all the basic ingredients: Great Lakes salmon and Smits Farms dill, plus pumpernickel bread and honey for the sauce. Experiment with additional flavorings such as vodka, aquavit, fennel, and caraway seed.
—**Elizabeth Richter, Green City Market board member**

FOR THE GRAVLAX:

1 (1½-to-2 pound) center-cut salmon fillet, skin on

½ cup brown sugar

¼ cup kosher salt (table salt will make gravlax too salty)

1 tablespoon crushed black or white peppercorns

2 bunches fresh dill

Pumpernickel bread, for serving

FOR THE HONEY MUSTARD–DILL SAUCE (MAKES ABOUT ¾ CUP):

⅓ cup sunflower or olive oil

¼ cup Dijon mustard

3 tablespoons chopped fresh dill

2 tablespoons honey

2 tablespoons white wine vinegar

1 teaspoon mustard powder

Prep time: 20 minutes

Marinating time: up to 4 days

Makes 24 servings

TO MAKE THE GRAVLAX:

1. Cut the salmon fillet into 2 equal-sized pieces that fit together like a sandwich. Using a pair of tweezers, remove any pin bones. Rinse the salmon and pat it dry with paper towels.

2. In a small bowl, combine the brown sugar, salt, and peppercorns.

3. Place 1 salmon fillet, skin side down, in a shallow glass baking dish. Spread ½ of the brown sugar–salt mixture over the salmon and top with 1 bunch of the fresh dill. Spread the remaining salt mixture over the dill. Place the other salmon fillet, skin side up, over the dill mixture.

4. Cover the dish tightly with plastic wrap and weigh it down with heavy jars or cans. Refrigerate for 2 to 4 days, turning the salmon "sandwich" over every 12 hours and basting with any liquid that accumulates as the salmon cures.

5. To serve, scrape and discard the salt mixture from the salmon. Rinse the salmon with cold water and pat dry with paper towels. Slice thinly on the bias against the skin. Arrange the slices on a platter lined with the remaining bunch of dill and serve with the bread and the Honey Mustard–Dill Sauce.

TO MAKE THE HONEY MUSTARD–DILL SAUCE:

1. Combine all the ingredients and mix well.

Red Kuri Squash Soup

Also called Japanese squash, red kuri squash looks like a pumpkin but without the deep ridges, and it has a slightly sweeter, almost nutty taste. Like other winter squash varieties, kuri squash matures about 3 months after blooming. While I often enjoy this squash roasted simply with butter and herbs, this soup is a twist on the more traditional butternut squash version.
—**Beth Eccles, farmer, Green Acres Farm; Green City Market board member**

1 large red kuri squash (2 to 2½ pounds)
Extra virgin olive oil, as needed
1 small apple, peeled, chopped
1 small onion, chopped
1 small fennel bulb, chopped
1 clove garlic, chopped
2 cups chicken stock or broth

1 bay leaf
12 sage leaves
Sea salt, to taste
Freshly ground black pepper, to taste
½ cup chopped pecans, toasted, for serving
Freshly grated cheese of your choice, as
   needed, for serving

Prep time: 30 minutes

Cook time: 55 minutes

Makes about 4 servings

1. Preheat the oven to 400°F.

2. Cut the squash crosswise in half and scrape out and discard the seed cavity. Cut each piece of squash in half again, making 4 pieces.

3. Place the squash pieces in a baking dish large enough to hold all of them in a single layer. Rub the flesh of the squash with a little of the oil. Cover the dish with foil and bake for 40 to 45 minutes, until tender. Remove from the oven. When the squash is cool enough to handle, carefully scoop the flesh away from the skin and place it in a bowl. Discard the skin.

4. In a large saucepan over medium heat, warm 2 tablespoons of the oil. Add the apple, onion, fennel, and garlic and sauté for 10 minutes. Add the stock, squash, and bay leaf. Cover and simmer for 40 minutes, until the vegetables are very tender.

Continued

5. While the soup is simmering, warm 1 tablespoon of the oil in a small skillet over medium heat. Add the sage leaves and sauté for 5 to 10 seconds on each side, until bright green and crispy. Remove from the heat and transfer the sage leaves to a plate lined with paper towels. (Microwave method: Paint the sage leaves with the oil on both sides and place them on a microwave-safe plate. Microwave at high power for 1 minute to 1 minute 15 seconds, until the leaves are crisp.)

6. Remove the saucepan from the heat. Remove and discard the bay leaf. Transfer the soup to a blender (or use an immersion [stick] blender) to purée it.

7. Season the soup with the salt and black pepper. The soup will be thick. Thin the soup with additional stock if desired. Ladle the soup into bowls and serve garnished with the pecans, sage leaves, cheese, and a drizzle of the oil.

Chestnut Soup with Bacon and Rosemary

On a cold winter day, this creamy soup is so warm and comforting. The addition of the chestnuts adds a subtle richness that plays wonderfully with the bacon. I like to garnish the soup with fresh sage leaves fried in olive oil. Green City Market is always inspiring our dishes at Vie and Perennial Virant. Each new season brings wonderful new ingredients. During the late fall and into early winter, Hillside Orchards always comes through with such tasty chestnuts; I felt this soup was the perfect way to showcase its product.

—Paul Virant, chef/partner, Vie Restaurant and Perennial Virant

---

¼ pound sliced bacon, diced
1 stalk celery, sliced
1 large carrot, sliced
1 large onion, chopped
2 tablespoons chopped fresh rosemary

1 pound shelled chestnuts
1 bay leaf
4 cups chicken stock or broth
½ cup heavy cream

Prep time: 20 minutes

Cook time: 25 minutes

Makes 6 servings

1. In a large saucepan over medium heat, cook the bacon, stirring occasionally, until crisp. Use a slotted spoon to transfer the bacon to a plate lined with paper towels and set aside.

2. Add the celery, carrot, and onion to the saucepan and sauté for 5 minutes. Add the rosemary and chestnuts and sauté for 2 minutes.

3. Raise the heat to high and add the bay leaf and stock. Bring to a boil. Reduce the heat to medium and simmer for 20 minutes, stirring occasionally, until the chestnuts and vegetables are tender. Remove from the heat and remove and discard the bay leaf.

4. Transfer the soup to a blender (or use an immersion [stick] blender) to purée it. Stir in the cream. Return to medium heat and warm the soup until it is heated through. Remove from the heat.

5. Ladle the soup into shallow bowls and serve topped with the bacon.

Butternut Squash Enchiladas with Mole Sauce

At my restaurant, we make this delicious dish for vegetarians and non-vegetarians alike. The nutritional content in the butternut squash is amazing, and the bittersweet, spicy mole sauce pairs well with the more savory filling. —**Maria Concannon, owner, Don Juan's Ristorante**

FOR THE SQUASH:

1 large butternut squash (2½ to 3 pounds)
2 tablespoons organic unsalted butter, melted
1 teaspoon salt
½ teaspoon ground cinnamon
¼ teaspoon freshly ground black pepper

FOR THE MOLE SAUCE:

2 cups boiling water
4 large dried ancho chilies
3 dried chipotle chilies
¼ cup slivered almonds
1 tablespoon tahini or peanut butter
½ cup chopped yellow onion
4 garlic cloves, peeled
4 whole plum tomatoes, seeded, coarsely chopped

¼ cup golden raisins
2 cups organic vegetable stock or broth, divided
1 tablespoon sunflower or vegetable oil
2 teaspoons ground cumin
1 teaspoon ground cinnamon
½ teaspoon ground allspice
Salt, to taste
Freshly ground black pepper, to taste

FOR THE ENCHILADAS:

Sunflower or vegetable oil, as needed
12 corn tortillas
1½ cups crumbled queso fresco cheese
Sour cream or crema, for serving
Chopped fresh cilantro, for serving

Prep time: 40 minutes

Cook time:
mole sauce, 1 hour
enchiladas, 30 minutes

Makes 6 servings

TO MAKE THE SQUASH:

1. Preheat the oven to 400°F.

2. Slice the squash in half. Scoop out and discard the seeds.

3. Place the squash halves, cut side up, in a casserole dish and add water to a depth of ¼ inch to the dish. Cover the dish with foil and bake for 35 to 45 minutes, until the squash is very tender. Remove from the oven.

4. Using a potholder to hold each half, scoop the squash pulp into a medium bowl and mash it with a potato masher. Stir in the butter, salt, cinnamon, and black pepper and set aside.

TO MAKE THE MOLE SAUCE:

1. Pour boiling water over chilies in a medium bowl and let stand for 15 minutes, until softened. Drain the chilies and discard the stems and seeds. Coarsely chop the chilies.

2. Place the chilies, almonds, tahini, onion, garlic, tomatoes, and raisins in a blender with 1 cup of the vegetable stock. Blend to a fairly smooth purée.

3. In a large saucepan or sauté pan over medium heat, warm the oil. Add the purée, cumin, cinnamon, and allspice and stir to combine. Sauté for 5 minutes. Add the remaining vegetable stock and bring to a simmer.

4. Reduce the heat to low and simmer for 1 hour, until thickened (the yield should be about 3 cups). Season with the salt and black pepper.

TO MAKE THE ENCHILADAS:

1. Preheat the oven to 350°F.

2. Spread ¾ cup of the Mole Sauce into a 13 × 9-inch glass baking dish.

3. In a small skillet over medium–high heat, warm enough oil to fill the skillet's bottom by a depth of ½ inch until hot. Quickly dip both sides of 1 tortilla in the hot oil to soften it and transfer to a plate lined with paper towels. Repeat until all the tortillas have been softened.

4. Fill 1 tortilla with ⅓ cup of the squash mixture. Roll up the tortilla and place it, seam side down, over the Mole Sauce in the baking dish. Repeat until all the tortillas have been filled and set in the baking dish, side by side.

5. Cover the enchiladas with the remaining Mole Sauce and cover the dish with foil. Bake for 30 minutes, until heated through. Remove from the oven. Uncover and top with the cheese. Let stand for 5 minutes.

6. Serve hot, garnished with the sour cream and cilantro.

Red Cabbage with Apples and Bacon

Serve this winter dish to brighten up roast chicken, pork, salmon, or just about any seasonal entrée. It may be prepared ahead and reheated just before serving. I love the colors of the red cabbage and apples, and the sweet and savory flavors are delicious.
—**Dana Benigno, former executive director, Green City Market**

---

2 thick slices bacon, chopped
1 small onion, chopped
4 cups chopped red cabbage
1 tablespoon balsamic vinegar

¾ teaspoon salt or more to taste
¼ teaspoon freshly ground black pepper
2 tart apples, such as Honeycrisp or Granny Smith, chopped

Prep time: 20 minutes
Cook time: 20 minutes
Makes 8 ½-cup servings

1. In a large, deep skillet over medium heat, sauté the bacon and onion for 6 minutes, until the onion is softened and the bacon is beginning to crisp at the edges. Add the cabbage and sauté for 6 to 8 minutes, until tender. Stir in the vinegar, salt, and black pepper.

2. Stir in the apples and sauté for 5 to 6 minutes, until the apples are heated through and crisp-tender. Remove from the heat.

3. Transfer to a bowl and serve immediately or chill for later use.

Greek Chicken and Potatoes

Just writing this favorite recipe makes my mouth water. Ingredients are few and preparation is easy for this healthful, savory dish that showcases our wonderful chicken. I have never served it to anyone who didn't want seconds. —**Jeanne Sexton, farmer, Meadow Haven Farm**

1 chicken (about 4 pounds), cut up, neck and back saved to make stock

4 medium baking potatoes (about 2 pounds),* skins on

⅓ cup fresh lemon juice

¼ cup olive oil

8 to 12 cloves garlic, peeled, chopped

2 tablespoons chopped fresh or 2 teaspoons dried oregano

1 teaspoon sea salt or more to taste

Freshly ground black pepper, to taste (optional)

Prep time: 25 minutes

Cook time: 1 hour

Makes 6 servings

1. Preheat the oven to 375°F.

2. Arrange the chicken pieces on a large, rimmed baking sheet (12 × 17 inch) or 2 smaller rimmed baking sheets.

3. Scrub the potatoes and cut each into 6 wedges. Arrange the wedges, peel side down, around the chicken pieces.

4. Combine the lemon juice, oil, and garlic and mix well. Brush ½ of the lemon mixture over the chicken and potatoes.

5. Bake for 30 minutes. Brush the remaining lemon mixture over the chicken and potatoes and top with the oregano. Sprinkle the salt over the chicken and potatoes. Continue baking for 30 minutes, until the chicken is cooked through and the potatoes are tender. Remove from the oven and season with the black pepper, if using.

6. Transfer the chicken and potatoes to a platter and serve hot.

* Or use 2 baking potatoes and 2 sweet potatoes

Turkey Meatloaf with Tomato Preserves

This turkey meatloaf is a great go-to dish for busy families. It's delicious, easy to make, and, when paired with seasonal vegetables, makes a nutritious dish for kids. Getting fresh ground turkey from TJ's Free-Range Poultry at Green City Market guarantees that the turkey was raised humanely and without the use of antibiotics. The Tomato Mountain Farm tomato preserves left over from the summer's harvest are a perfect topping for the meatloaf, adding flavor and color. Serve with a seasonal vegetable or sautéed spinach.
—**Diane Schmidt, customer**

---

3 tablespoons olive oil
1 cup finely chopped onion
1 cup finely chopped celery
1½ pounds ground turkey
2 large eggs
1 cup fresh breadcrumbs

3 tablespoons chopped fresh or
   1 tablespoon dried thyme leaves
1 teaspoon salt
1 teaspoon freshly ground black pepper
⅓ cup tomato preserves

Prep time: 30 minutes

Cook time: 55 minutes

Makes 6 servings

1. Preheat the oven to 350°F. Grease a 9 × 5-inch loaf pan with a little of the oil.

2. In a large skillet or sauté pan over medium heat, warm the oil. Add the onion and sauté for 5 minutes. Add the celery and sauté for 5 minutes. Remove from the heat.

3. Transfer the mixture to a large bowl and set aside to cool for 10 minutes.

4. Add the turkey, eggs, breadcrumbs, thyme, salt, and black pepper to the bowl and mix well.

5. Spoon the mixture into the prepared loaf pan and smooth the top with a spatula. Spread the preserves evenly over the turkey mixture.

6. Bake for 50 to 55 minutes, until the internal temperature reaches 165°F. Remove from the oven. Serve hot.

Not-So-Scary Spare Ribs

A recipe for oven-baked pork spare ribs is a must-have Midwest staple. Some people are intimidated by the idea of cooking ribs, but this is an easy and tasty dish everyone will love. On those not-so-cold days, try finishing the cooked ribs on the grill, taking care to brush them with a little barbecue sauce and cooking for about 5 minutes per side.
—**Lou Ann Robinson, farmer, Jake's Country Meats**

1 large rack spare ribs (about 2½ pounds)
3 cloves garlic, minced
1 teaspoon seasoned salt or salt

½ teaspoon freshly ground black pepper
¼ teaspoon cayenne pepper
1½ cups apple cider or juice

Prep time: 15 minutes
Cook time: 2 hours
Makes 3 to 4 servings

1. Preheat the oven to 350°F.

2. Place the ribs in a shallow roasting pan, bone side down. Evenly sprinkle the ribs with the garlic, salt, black pepper, and cayenne pepper. Pour the apple cider over the ribs. Cover with foil.

3. Bake for 2 hours, until the meat is very tender when tested with a sharp knife. Remove from the oven. Cut into individual serving pieces.

4. Serve warm immediately, or finish on the grill as noted above.

Hearty Elk Chili

We like to ask our customers for recipes that showcase our lean ground elk. Here is a recipe we collected last year from Southwest: The Beautiful Cookbook *and adapted to make our own. The chili will keep in the refrigerator for 4 days or in the freezer for 3 months.*
—**Joel Espe, farmer, Hawks Hill Elk Ranch**

2 tablespoons vegetable oil

2 cups chopped onions

2 red bell peppers, diced

2 large poblano or Anaheim chili peppers, chopped

4 cloves garlic, minced

2 pounds ground elk meat

1 (32-ounce) jar organic crushed tomatoes

2 teaspoons ground cumin

2 teaspoons dried oregano

1½ teaspoons salt, plus more to taste

½ teaspoon cayenne pepper, plus more to taste

½ cup water

¼ cup cornmeal

Shredded Cheddar cheese, as needed, for garnish (optional)

Sour cream, as needed, for garnish (optional)

Chopped green onions, as needed, for garnish (optional)

Chopped cilantro, as needed, for garnish (optional)

Prep time: 20 minutes

Cook time: 1 hour

Makes 6 to 8 servings

1. In a large saucepan or Dutch oven over medium heat, warm the oil. Add the onions and sauté for 5 minutes. Add the bell peppers, chili peppers, and garlic and sauté for 5 minutes.

2. Add the elk meat to the saucepan and cook, stirring occasionally, for 5 to 6 minutes, until browned.

3. Raise the heat to high and stir in the tomatoes, cumin, oregano, salt, and cayenne pepper. Bring to a boil.

4. Reduce the heat to low, cover, and cook, stirring once, for 30 minutes.

5. In a small bowl, combine the water and cornmeal with a whisk. Stir the cornmeal slurry into the chili. Simmer, uncovered, for 30 minutes. Remove from the heat.

6. Taste and season again with the salt and cayenne pepper, if desired. Ladle the chili into shallow bowls and serve garnished with the cheese, sour cream, green onions, and cilantro, if using.

Radical Root Vegetable and Beef Stew

This is my go-to stew recipe that I make the minute it turns cold outside. The best part about it is making use of all the celeriac, turnips, and carrots we have in abundance in the fall and early winter. I really enjoy the meaty flavor of the root vegetables when simmered in the wine and broth. —**Alison Parker, farmer, Radical Root Organic Farm**

1 large celeriac (celery root), cut into
    1½-inch pieces

2 large carrots, cut into ½-inch pieces

8 ounces small potatoes, cut into
    1½-inch pieces

2 small turnips or 1 large turnip, cut into
    1½-inch pieces

8 ounces Brussels sprouts, halved or quartered

1 large onion, cut into 1½-inch pieces

3 tablespoons olive oil, divided

2 pounds beef stew meat

½ teaspoon salt, plus more to taste

½ teaspoon freshly ground black pepper,
    plus more to taste

1 cup dry red wine

4 cups beef broth or stock

3 sprigs fresh thyme

Chopped fresh thyme leaves, for sprinkling
    (optional)

Prep time: 30 minutes

Cook time: 1½ hours

Makes 6 to 8 servings

1. Preheat the oven to 375°F.

2. Place the celeriac, carrots, potatoes, turnips, Brussels sprouts, and onion in a large bowl and drizzle on 2 tablespoons of the oil. Toss well.

3. Arrange the vegetables in a shallow roasting pan. Bake for 30 to 35 minutes, stirring after 15 minutes, until browned. Remove from the oven and reduce the oven temperature to 325°F.

4. In an ovenproof Dutch oven or large saucepan over medium heat, warm the remaining 1 tablespoon of oil. Add the meat and cook for 5 minutes on each side, until brown. Add the wine to the Dutch oven and cook for 4 to 5 minutes, stirring occasionally, until the wine is reduced by half. Remove from the heat.

5. Add the browned vegetables, beef broth, and thyme sprigs to the Dutch oven. Cover the Dutch oven and bake in the oven for 1½ hours, until the meat is fork tender.

6. Using a large slotted spoon, transfer the meat and vegetables to a large bowl. Discard the thyme sprigs. Cover with foil to keep warm.

7. Place the Dutch oven containing the broth mixture over medium heat. Cook for 10 to 12 minutes, until the mixture is reduced to the desired thickness to use as a sauce. Remove from the heat.

8. Return the meat and vegetables to the Dutch oven. Taste and season again with the salt and black pepper, if desired.

9. Transfer to the same large serving bowl and serve garnished with thyme leaves, if desired.

Not Your Aunt Ruthie's Brisket

Green City Market was one of the first places Jason Hammel and Amalea Tshilds took me when I first moved to Chicago and started working at their first restaurant, Lula Café. Over the last nine years, the Market has become a fixture in my life. The farmers have become friends, the patrons have become my customers, and I've exchanged many ideas for seasonal cooking with other chefs. It is a wonderful community and I am happy to be a part of it. For this recipe, I prefer brisket that has some texture. The roasting process renders off a lot of fat and tightens up the leanness of the meat so you can still eat it like a steak even after it's braised. —**Jason Vincent, chef de cuisine, Nightwood Restaurant**

---

1 whole (5-pound) beef brisket, untrimmed
3 tablespoons kosher salt
1 tablespoon garlic powder
1 tablespoon onion powder
1 tablespoon dried dill
1 tablespoon smoked paprika

1 tablespoon ground ginger
1 cup ketchup
1 quart (4 cups) whole milk
1 large onion, coarsely chopped
1 orange, quartered
2 teaspoons fish sauce

Prep time: 20 minutes
Marinating time: overnight
Cook time: 3 to 4 hours
Makes 8 to 10 servings

1. Trim most of the fat from the brisket, leaving only a thin layer.

2. In a small bowl, combine the salt, garlic powder, onion powder, dill, paprika, and ginger. Rub the spice mixture over both sides of the brisket. Wrap the brisket tightly in plastic wrap and refrigerate overnight, or at least for 12 hours.

3. Preheat the oven to 450°F.

4. Place the brisket on a rack in a large, deep roasting pan. Spread the ketchup over the top of the brisket. Roast for 1 hour (you may wish to open a window, as roasting the brisket for this long at that high a temperature could generate some smoke). The top should appear caramelized when it's ready.

5. Remove the brisket from the oven, transfer it to a baking sheet, and set it aside to rest. Reduce the oven temperature to 250°F.

Continued

6. Add the milk to the drippings in the roasting pan and mix well. Add the onion, orange, and fish sauce to the pan and mix well. Place the brisket in the roasting pan with the liquid and cover the pan tightly with foil.

7. Return the roasting pan to the oven and continue roasting for 2 to 3 hours, until the brisket is fork tender. Uncover the pan and let the brisket stand in the liquid until it cools to room temperature. Transfer the brisket to a carving board and discard the liquid.

8. Slice the brisket against the grain into thin slices. Serve on a serving platter.

Apple Cider-Brined Chicken

Cider makes excellent brine for chicken and pork because of its sweetness and hints of apple. I developed this recipe while preparing for a demo at Green City Market. I served it with mashed potatoes spiked with apple cider, butter, and sage. Do not reduce the salt amount the recipe calls for, because the salt helps infuse the apple cider flavor into the bird. If you are brining a cut-up chicken, soak it in the brine for only 4 hours. If you would like to use the brine for a turkey, double the amount used. —**Peter Klein, farmer, Seedling Farms**

3 cups water
⅓ cup kosher salt
2 bay leaves
2 cloves garlic, peeled and smashed

Favorite herb sprigs (optional)
4 cups apple cider
1 (3½-to-4 pound) chicken

Prep time: 20 minutes
Chill time: 24 hours
Cook time: 1 hour
Standing time: 10 minutes
Makes 4 to 6 servings

1. In a medium saucepan over high heat, bring the water and salt just to a boil, stirring to dissolve the salt. Remove from the heat and add the bay leaves, the garlic, and the herbs, if using. Stir in the cider and allow to cool to room temperature.

2. Place the chicken in a 2-gallon plastic food storage bag and pour the brine over chicken. Seal the bag and refrigerate for 24 hours, turning the bag over once.

3. Preheat the oven to 375°F.

4. Remove the chicken from the brine and discard the brine. Place the chicken, breast side up, on a rack in a shallow roasting pan.

5. Roast the chicken for 30 minutes. Check the chicken to make sure it is not browning too quickly. If so, cover loosely with foil.

6. Continue roasting the chicken for 25 to 30 minutes, until its internal temperature (taken in the thigh) registers 160°F. Remove from the oven and let stand 10 minutes before carving.

Roasted Parsnips and Sweet Potatoes with Caper Vinaigrette

On May 4, 2013, the opening day of Green City Market, I saw these gorgeous parsnips from Green Acres Farm. Farmer Beth Eccles told me that the parsnips had been left in the ground over the winter. Frost activates the root vegetables' natural sugars, making them taste very sweet. What I love about the Market is that you can find special produce that isn't available anywhere else and hear directly from the farmers why the produce is so unique. It's easy to create beautiful and delicious meals using ingredients from our local farms. You can change this recipe to use other favorite vegetables like carrots, beets, or cauliflower. (Adapted from Plenty *by Yotam Ottolenghi, Chronicle Books LLC, 2011.)*
—**Kathy Paddor, Green City Market board member**

---

4 large parsnips (about 1½ pounds), peeled

4 medium red onions

6 tablespoons olive oil, divided

1½ teaspoons kosher salt, divided

1 teaspoon freshly ground black pepper, divided

2 medium sweet potatoes (about 1¼ pounds)

1 whole head of garlic, halved horizontally

30 cherry tomatoes, halved

2 tablespoons fresh lemon juice

1½ teaspoons pure maple syrup

½ teaspoon Dijon mustard

3 to 4 tablespoons drained small capers

3 tablespoons chopped fresh herbs, such as thyme, rosemary, and parsley

---

Prep time: 25 minutes

Cook time: 50 minutes

Makes 4 to 6 servings

1. Preheat the oven to 375°F.

2. Cut the parsnips crosswise and then lengthwise into 2- × ½-inch sticks. Cut each onion into six wedges. Place the parsnips and onions in a medium bowl. Drizzle them with 2 tablespoons of the oil and sprinkle with 1 teaspoon of the salt and ½ teaspoon of the black pepper. Toss well.

3. Spread the parsnips and onions in a single layer in a large, shallow roasting pan. Bake for 20 minutes.

4. While the parsnips and onions are baking, scrub but do not peel the sweet potatoes. Cut them into thin wedges and cut the wedges into 2-inch pieces. Place the sweet potatoes in the same bowl used to toss the vegetables. Add the garlic and toss with 2 tablespoons of the oil.

5. Remove the roasting pan from the oven and add the sweet potato mixture to the parsnips and onions. Toss well. Return to the oven and bake for 20 to 25 minutes, until the vegetables are tender, adding the cherry tomatoes to the pan during the last 5 minutes of baking time.

6. While the vegetables are baking, in a medium bowl whisk together the lemon juice and the remaining 2 tablespoons of oil. Whisk in the maple syrup, the mustard, and the remaining ½ teaspoon each of salt and black pepper. Stir in the capers. Set aside.

7. Remove the roasting pan from the oven and transfer the contents to a serving bowl. Squeeze the garlic cloves out of their papery skins and into the bowl; discard the skins.

8. Pour the vinaigrette over the vegetables. Add the fresh herbs and toss well. Serve immediately.

Fingerling Potatoes and Garlicky Swiss Chard with Ricotta Cheese

PICTURED ON PAGE 172

The inspiration for this dish came from my love of all the varieties of potatoes and greens available at the Market. Although I usually use spinach in this dish, it can easily be replaced by any other greens, depending on availability. The ricotta cheese adds a nice richness to the dish, and who doesn't like roasted garlic and fresh chives? Almost everything used here can be found at Green City Market or any other local source. The dish is great all year round as a side or vegetarian option. —**Peter Stasiulis, customer**

FOR THE HOMEMADE RICOTTA CHEESE
(makes 1½ cups; you will need only
½ cup for this recipe):

1 gallon whole milk

½ gallon heavy whipping cream

½ cup distilled white vinegar, divided

FOR THE FINGERLING POTATOES AND
GARLICKY SWISS CHARD:

1 whole head garlic

5 tablespoons olive oil, divided

**1 pound heirloom fingerling potatoes,
scrubbed**

1 teaspoon salt

½ teaspoon freshly ground black pepper

**2 bunches Swiss chard or 1½ pounds fresh
spinach leaves**

**½ cup market whole milk ricotta cheese
(or see recipe below)**

**2 tablespoons chopped fresh thyme leaves,
for sprinkling**

2 tablespoons chopped chives, for sprinkling

Prep time: 40 minutes

Cook time: 1 hour 25 minutes

Makes 4 servings

TO MAKE THE HOMEMADE RICOTTA CHEESE:

1. In a large saucepan or Dutch oven over medium-low heat, combine the milk and cream. Add ¼ cup of the vinegar and bring to a simmer. Cook for 2 to 3 minutes, until curds form (if curds fail to form, add the other ¼ cup vinegar).

2. Once the mixture nears the boiling point, remove from the heat, cover, and let stand for 30 minutes.

3. Strain the mixture through a cheesecloth-lined colander and discard the whey liquid. Place the colander over a bowl and allow it to drain. Place in the refrigerator for at least 1 hour.

4. Once the ricotta is fully drained, remove it from the cheesecloth and transfer it to a tightly sealed container. Keep chilled until ready to use or serve.

TO MAKE THE FINGERLING POTATOES AND GARLICKY SWISS CHARD:

1. Preheat the oven to 375°F.

2. Cut off the top of the head of garlic, exposing the cloves. Place the head on a small sheet of foil and drizzle 1 tablespoon of the oil over the top. Tightly wrap the foil around the garlic, covering it completely. Roast it in the oven for 30 minutes.

3. While the garlic is roasting, cut the potatoes on the bias into ½-inch-thick slices and place them on a large, rimmed baking sheet. Drizzle 2 tablespoons of the oil and sprinkle the salt and black pepper over the potatoes. Toss well.

4. When the 30 minutes are up for the garlic, place the baking sheet containing the potatoes in the oven with the garlic. Continue baking for 20 to 25 minutes, until the potatoes are lightly browned and tender and the garlic cloves are very tender. Remove from the oven and set aside.

5. Thinly slice the Swiss chard stalks and cut the leaves into thick strips. (If using spinach, cut its leaves into strips and discard its thick stems.)

6. In a large, deep skillet over medium heat, warm the remaining 2 tablespoons of oil. Unwrap the garlic head and squeeze the softened garlic cloves from the skins into the skillet; discard the skins. Add the chard stems to the skillet and sauté for 4 to 5 minutes. Add the chard leaves and sauté until just wilted. (If using the spinach, add in batches and turn the leaves with tongs until they are wilted.) Remove from the heat and season with the salt and black pepper.

7. Arrange the potatoes on four serving plates and top with the chard. Spoon the ricotta cheese over the chard. Sprinkle the thyme leaves and chives over the ricotta cheese and serve.

Fingerling Potatoes and Garlicky Swiss Chard with Ricotta Cheese
Recipe on page 170

Maple-Glazed Breakfast Bread
Recipe on page 174

Maple-Glazed Breakfast Bread

PICTURED ON PAGE 173

This hearty breakfast bread is a wonderful combination of sweet and savory. The bacon adds richness enhanced by the Cheddar cheese and balanced by the sweet maple glaze. On top of being satisfying and delicious, it's incredibly easy to make and keeps very well for subsequent meals. —**Tim Burton, farmer, Burton's Maplewood Farm**

FOR THE BREAD:

2 tablespoons unsalted butter
¾ cup milk
1 packet (1 tablespoon) active dry yeast
2 large eggs
2 cups all-purpose flour
2 tablespoons pure maple syrup
1 teaspoon baking soda

1 tablespoon kosher salt
1½ cups shredded Cheddar cheese
1 pound bacon, cooked crisp, crumbled
¼ cup minced fresh chives

FOR THE GLAZE:

6 tablespoons confectioners' sugar
3 tablespoons pure maple syrup

Prep time: 15 minutes
Rising time: 45 minutes
Cook time: 35 minutes
Makes 16 (½-inch-thick) slices

TO MAKE THE BREAD:

1. In a medium saucepan over low heat, melt the butter. Add the milk and cook until the temperature measured with an instant-read or candy thermometer reaches 110°F. Remove from the heat.

2. Pour the heated milk into the bowl of a stand mixer fitted with the whisk attachment. Sprinkle the yeast over the milk. Stir and let stand for 5 minutes.

3. Add the eggs to the bowl and beat on low speed until blended. Add the flour, maple syrup, baking soda, and salt and beat on low speed until well blended (the batter will be slightly stiff). Remove the bowl from the mixer.

4. Add the Cheddar cheese, bacon, and chives to the batter. Knead the dough with your hands for 2 to 3 minutes and form a loaf.

5. Press the loaf into a greased 9 × 5-inch loaf pan. Cover and let rise in a warm place for 40 to 45 minutes, until doubled in size.

6. Preheat the oven to 375°F.

7. Bake for 30 to 35 minutes, until golden brown. Turn the loaf out onto a wire rack and allow to cool to room temperature.

TO MAKE THE GLAZE:

1. In a small bowl, combine the confectioners' sugar and syrup and mix until smooth.

2. Pour the glaze over the cooled loaf. Slice and serve.

Sweet Potato Latkes

Here's a fun variation of a traditional potato pancake, or latke, *as it's called in the Jewish cooking tradition. You can adapt this recipe to a more savory flavor by adding leeks and removing the cinnamon. This is perfect for serving during Hanukkah or any time you're craving a comforting, tasty appetizer; a side dish; or even a light lunch.*
—**Cindy Kurman, Green City Market board member**

---

5 cups grated, peeled, raw sweet potatoes

2 large eggs

¼ cup matzo meal or all-purpose flour

2 tablespoons minced onion

1 teaspoon ground cinnamon

½ teaspoon sea salt

½ teaspoon freshly ground black pepper

Sunflower oil or canola oil, for frying

Prep time: 20 minutes

Cook time: 25 minutes

Makes 6 servings
(2 latkes each)

1. In a large bowl, combine all the ingredients, except the oil, and stir until combined.

2. In a large nonstick skillet over medium–low heat, warm 2 tablespoons of the oil. Check to ensure it is ready for frying by adding a drop of water; if it sizzles, it's ready.

3. For each latke, drop a scant ¼ cup of the sweet potato mixture into the skillet. Make sure that you do not crowd the latkes in the skillet. Press down on each piece of the mixture gently with a spatula, forming them into little cakes.

4. Cook for 3 to 4 minutes on each side, until the cakes are golden brown and the potatoes are cooked in the center. As the latkes are cooked, remove them from the skillet and place them on a plate lined with paper towels to remove any excess oil. Once each latke has been blotted, transfer it to a serving platter. Keep the platter warm in a 200°F oven while you make the remaining batches.

5. Repeat until all of the latke batter has been used, adding additional oil to the skillet as needed for remaining batches. Remove the skillet from the heat.

6. Remove the platter from the oven and serve hot.

Potato and Turnip Gratin

Abby Mandel, the founder of Green City Market, loved having company over for informal dinners at which she would arrange beautiful platters of food on her kitchen island so people could help themselves to the season's bounty. This gratin was inspired by a trip to France where Abby noticed that chefs would layer various root vegetables, such as turnips or kohlrabi, along with potatoes in their gratins. —**Chris Djuric, customer and assistant to the Mandel family**

2 tablespoons organic unsalted butter, divided

3 cloves garlic, minced, divided

1 cup heavy cream

2 pounds turnips or 1 large kohlrabi, peeled

2 pounds russet potatoes, peeled

Salt, to taste

Freshly ground black pepper, to taste

1 large leek, white part only, thinly sliced, divided

1 cup shredded Gouda cheese or another good melting cheese, divided

1 slice whole-wheat bread, torn into pieces

Prep time: 30 minutes

Cook time: 1 hour

Standing time: 15 minutes

Makes 6 servings

1. Preheat the oven to 375°F.

2. Place 1 tablespoon of the butter and ½ the minced garlic in the bottom of a 2-quart, shallow, microwave-safe casserole dish. Microwave on high power for 30 seconds, until the butter is melted. Remove from the microwave.

3. Brush the butter mixture around the dish, lightly coating the bottom and sides. Set aside.

4. Combine the cream and remaining garlic in a small measuring cup and set aside.

5. Place the turnips on a microwave-safe plate and microwave on high power for 4 minutes. Remove from the microwave and set aside to cool.

6. Using a large, sharp knife or mandoline, thinly slice the turnips and potatoes into ⅛-inch-thick pieces. Place the slices of each vegetable in separate bowls.

7. Pour ¼ cup of the cream mixture over each bowl of vegetables. Toss well and season generously with the salt and black pepper. Toss again.

8. Arrange ½ the potatoes in the prepared casserole dish. Top with ½ of the leek and ¼ cup of the cheese.

9. For the next layer, use all of the turnips, the remaining leek, and ¼ cup of the cheese.

10. For the last layer, use all of the remaining potatoes and the remaining ½ cup of cheese. Pour the remaining cream mixture evenly over the top.

11. Place the bread pieces in the bowl of a food processor. Pulse until the breadcrumbs reach the desired coarseness.

12. In a small skillet over medium heat, melt the remaining 1 tablespoon of butter. Add the breadcrumbs to the skillet and toss well. Remove from the heat.

13. Sprinkle the breadcrumbs over the casserole and cover the dish with foil. Place the dish on a baking sheet and bake for 45 minutes.

14. Uncover the dish and bake for 15 minutes, until the vegetables are tender. Let stand for 15 minutes before serving.

Black-Eyed Peas and Roasted Brussels Sprouts

The idea for this dish arose from a black-eyed pea salad we made for a catering client after one of our weekly trips to the Market. We thought the Brussels sprouts added a contrasting texture, and the rosemary evokes familiar flavors of winter. The sprouts are great as a side dish with roasted chicken or lamb. —**Debbie Sharpe, owner, Feast Restaurant and The Goddess and Grocer**

1 pound Brussels sprouts
2 cups chopped red onions
3 tablespoons olive oil, divided
2 teaspoons chopped fresh rosemary
½ teaspoon ground cumin
½ teaspoon salt

½ teaspoon freshly ground black pepper, plus more to taste
2 cups cooked black-eyed peas*
1 jalapeño pepper, seeded, minced
½ cup chopped parsley
2 tablespoons fresh lemon juice

Prep time: 15 minutes

Cook time: 15 minutes

Makes 4 to 6 servings

1. Preheat the oven to 400°F.

2. Quarter the Brussels sprouts and place them, along with the onions, on a large, rimmed baking sheet. Drizzle 1 tablespoon of the oil and sprinkle the cumin, salt, and black pepper over the Brussels sprouts and onions. Toss well.

3. Roast for 15 minutes, until browned and tender.

4. While the Brussels sprouts are roasting, combine the remaining ingredients, except the oil, in a large serving bowl and toss to combine.

5. Remove the baking sheet from the oven.

6. Add the remaining 2 tablespoons of oil to the serving bowl and toss well. Add the Brussels sprouts and onion to the bowl and toss well.

7. Season with additional black pepper, if desired, and serve immediately.

* To cook dried black-eyed peas, place them in a large Dutch oven or saucepan over high heat, cover them with water, and bring to a boil. Remove from the heat and let stand for 1 hour. Drain the black-eyed peas and return them to the Dutch oven over high heat. Cover again with water and bring to a boil. Reduce the heat to medium–low and simmer for 40 to 60 minutes, until tender. Drain the black-eyed peas and rinse them with cold water. Extra cooked black-eyed peas may be stored in the refrigerator up to 5 days.

Rosemary Shortbread Cookies

This simple cookie is my signature treat at holiday time, and it lends itself beautifully to any herb from the Market, including thyme or lavender. Scottish grandmothers swear that these cookies taste better when mixed by hand, so that's the way I do it. They make a lovely holiday or hostess gift. —**Janine MacLachlan, volunteer**

½ cup unsalted butter, room temperature
¼ cup sugar
1 teaspoon coarse sea salt, plus more
    for sprinkling

2 tablespoons minced fresh rosemary,
    plus more for sprinkling
1 cup all-purpose flour

Prep time: 15 minutes
Cook time: 35 minutes
Makes 16 servings

1. Preheat the oven to 325°F. Grease an 8-inch-square baking pan.

2. In a large bowl, cream together the butter, sugar, and salt until well combined. Stir in the rosemary. Add the flour and mix well. (The dough may become stiff, so be patient.)

3. Press the dough into the prepared baking pan. Sprinkle with a little of the extra salt and rosemary. Using a fork, pierce the dough at 1-inch intervals.

4. Bake for 30 to 35 minutes, until lightly golden around the edges. Remove from the oven and immediately cut the cookies into triangle shapes while still in the pan. Set aside to cool for 5 minutes.

5. Remove the cookies from the pan using an offset spatula or fork. Serve warm or at room temperature.

Maple Pecan Cookies

We like to make these rich, buttery cookies flavored with maple syrup and pecans in the winter because they remind us of little snowballs. We consider ourselves lucky to be able to work with Tracey Vowell's beautiful pecans (Three Sisters Garden) and Tim Burton's grade-B maple syrup (Burton's Maplewood Farm). Both of these ingredients really shine in this cookie. —**Sandra Holl, vendor, Floriole Café and Bakery**

---

2 cups pecan halves
8 ounces unsalted butter, softened to room
   temperature
1½ cups confectioners' sugar, divided
3 tablespoons pure maple syrup

1 teaspoon pure vanilla extract
1 teaspoon finely shredded orange zest
¼ teaspoon salt
2 cups all-purpose flour

Prep time: 30 minutes

Chill time: 30 minutes

Cook time: 14 to 16 minutes

Makes about 4 dozen cookies

1. Preheat the oven to 350°F. Line 2 baking sheets with parchment paper and set aside.

2. Place the pecans in a single layer on a separate rimmed baking sheet. Bake for 5 to 6 minutes, until the pecans are fragrant. Remove from the oven and allow to cool to room temperature.

3. Place the pecans in the bowl of a food processor. Pulse until the pecans are finely chopped, but not paste-like. Set aside.

4. In the bowl of a stand mixer, beat together the butter and ½ cup of the confectioners' sugar until light and fluffy.

5. Add the syrup, vanilla, orange zest, and salt to the bowl of the stand mixer and beat on low speed until well blended. Scrape down the sides of the bowl. Add the pecans and beat on low speed until well blended.

6. Add the flour to the bowl of the stand mixer and beat on low speed until a well-blended dough forms. Place the bowl of dough in the refrigerator to chill for at least 30 minutes, until the dough is firm.

Continued

7. Using a tablespoon measure, scoop out a level portion of dough and roll it into a ball. Place each dough ball 1 to 2 inches apart on the prepared baking sheets.

8. Bake for 14 to 16 minutes, until golden brown. Remove from the oven and set aside the cookies on wire racks to cool completely.

9. Place the remaining 1 cup of confectioners' sugar in a medium bowl. Toss each cookie until well coated.

10. Either serve or store in a tightly sealed container in the refrigerator for up to 1 week or in the freezer for up to 3 months. If desired, cookies may be tossed with more confectioners' sugar just before serving.

Roasted Delicata Squash and Brown Sugar Ice Cream

This is one of my favorite fall ice creams. Most people would use pumpkin in a recipe like this, but I prefer delicatas. They are easy to roast, and they have a wonderful creamy texture and sweet flavor. Best of all, all the dairy products, eggs and squash needed for the recipe can be bought directly from farmers at Green City Market.
—**Nancy Silver, vendor, Snookelfritz Ice Cream Artistry**

1 large or 2 small delicata squash
1 tablespoon canola oil
1¾ cups heavy cream
½ cup whole milk
1 cup packed light brown sugar, divided

1 vanilla bean, split open, scraped, and seeds and pod reserved
6 large egg yolks
¼ teaspoon ground cinnamon

Prep time: 45 minutes
Cooking time (squash): 45 minutes
Chill time: 2 hours
Makes about 3 cups

1. Preheat the oven to 375°F.

2. Slice the squash in ½ and scoop out and discard the seeds. Brush the halves lightly with the oil and place them on a rimmed baking sheet.

3. Roast the squash for 45 minutes, until tender. Remove from the oven and set aside to cool completely. Scoop out squash flesh, discarding skin.

4. Place the roasted squash in a blender or the bowl of a mini food processor. Process until puréed. Transfer to a bowl and place in the refrigerator to chill completely.

5. In a heavy-bottomed saucepan over medium heat, bring the cream, the milk, ½ cup of the brown sugar, the vanilla bean pod, and the reserved scraped seeds from inside the pod to just a simmer.

6. While the cream mixture is warming, whisk together the egg yolks, the cinnamon, and the remaining ½ cup of the brown sugar in a large bowl.

Continued

7. Remove the cream mixture from the heat and remove and discard the vanilla bean pod. Slowly temper the simmering cream mixture, 1 ladle at a time, into the egg mixture, whisking constantly.

8. Pour the combined mixture back into the saucepan and stir with a wooden spoon. Place the saucepan over medium–low heat and cook for 2 to 3 minutes, until the mixture is thickened and an instant-read thermometer inserted in the mixture reads 180°F. Remove from the heat and transfer the mixture back into the large bowl.

9. Whisk the chilled squash purée into the large bowl. Set aside and let stand for 10 minutes.

10. Strain the mixture through a chinois or other fine mesh strainer.* Place the bowl containing the mixture in the refrigerator and chill until cold, from 2 hours to overnight.

11. Transfer the mixture to an ice cream machine and proceed according to the manufacturer's instructions.

12. Serve immediately.

* For a smoother texture, purée the finished ice cream base in a blender for a few seconds before straining it.

Market Beet Cake

The Green City Market Beet Cake, as we refer to it at Limelight Catering, was first served at the Market's tenth anniversary celebration to the several hundred people in attendance—and it was an instant hit. Abby Mandel and Mayor Richard M. Daley and his wife, Maggie, were among the honored guests. At the event, Mayor Daley officially proclaimed that May 17, 2008, would be Green City Market Day. Abby had my husband record the song "The Loco-Motion" as "Local-Motion" for the event's parade. It's now a favorite among the kids in the Market's Club Sprouts!
—**Rita Gutekanst, principal, Limelight Catering; Green City Market board member**

---

3 large eggs

1½ cups sugar

2 teaspoons pure vanilla extract

2 cups all-purpose flour

2 teaspoons baking powder

1 teaspoon salt

1 cup sunflower or canola oil

1 cup grated raw peeled red beets

1 cup grated carrots

1 cup chopped pecans or walnuts, toasted

Cream cheese or buttercream frosting
   (optional)

Prep time: 25 minutes

Cook time: 1 hour 10 minutes

Makes 8 to 10 servings

1. Preheat the oven to 350°F. Grease a 9 × 5-inch loaf pan. (For easier removal of the cake, also line the bottom of the greased pan with parchment paper.)

2. Separate the egg yolks from the whites. Place the egg whites in the bowl of a stand mixer fitted with the whisk attachment or use a hand mixer. Beat the egg whites on low speed for 1 minute. Increase speed to medium-high and beat until they form stiff peaks, 2 to 3 minutes longer. Set aside.

3. In another large bowl, beat together the egg yolks, sugar, and vanilla.

4. In a medium bowl, combine the flour, baking powder, and salt.

5. Alternately add the oil and the flour mixture to the egg yolk mixture in thirds, beating until combined each time.

Continued

6. Using a wooden spoon, stir the beets, carrots, and nuts into the batter. Fold the stiff egg whites into the batter.

7. Spread the batter into the prepared loaf pan. Bake for 1 hour and 10 minutes, until the cake is browned and a wooden pick inserted in the center comes out clean. Remove from the oven.

8. Transfer the pan to a wire rack and let stand for 20 minutes.

9. Turn out the cake onto the rack and set it aside to cool completely. Spread the top of the cake with the frosting, if desired. Slice and serve.

Pear Streusel Coffee Cake

This is my favorite fast coffee cake recipe from my grandma Elsie, although she used apples. Inspired by trips to Green City Market, I saw some pears one day and just had to bake with them, so I swapped out the apples in this version. In addition to regularly shopping at the Market, I love helping out by giving cooking demonstrations, usually with my three kids Gio, Ruby, and Ella in tow to help. —**Gale Gand, chef and founding partner, Tru**

FOR THE CAKE BATTER:

1¼ cups all-purpose flour
½ cup sugar
2¼ teaspoons baking powder
½ teaspoon salt
½ teaspoon ground cinnamon
1 large egg, beaten
½ cup milk

¼ cup unsalted butter, melted
2 ripe pears (such as Bartlett), unpeeled, diced

FOR THE STREUSEL TOPPING:

½ cup sugar
¼ cup all-purpose flour
1 teaspoon ground cinnamon
3 tablespoons unsalted butter, melted

Prep time: 20 minutes
Cook time: 35 minutes
Makes 9 servings

TO MAKE THE CAKE BATTER:

1. Preheat the oven to 400°F. Grease an 8-inch baking dish or line it with parchment paper.

2. In a medium-sized bowl, combine the flour, sugar, baking powder, salt, and cinnamon. Using a wooden spoon, stir well. Add the egg, milk, and butter and stir until combined. Stir in the pears.

3. Pour the batter into the prepared dish.

TO MAKE THE STREUSEL TOPPING:

1. In a small bowl, combine the sugar, flour, and cinnamon and mix well. Add the butter, stirring until blended.

2. Sprinkle the streusel mixture over the cake batter in the baking dish.

TO BAKE THE CAKE:

1. Bake for 30 to 35 minutes, until golden brown. Remove from the oven.

2. Transfer the cake to a wire rack and let it cool completely.

3. Cut the cake into squares and serve. The cake keeps for up to 4 days, covered, at room temperature, and here's a tip: The cake is even better when made the night before serving.

Seasonal Shopping List

Spring

arugula
asparagus
basil
carrots
chives
dried beans
fiddleheads
garlic scapes
green garlic
green onions
kale
kohlrabi
leeks
lemongrass
lettuce
mint

morels
mushrooms
mustard greens
parsley
peas
radishes
ramps
rhubarb
snap peas
spinach
sprouts
stinging nettles
strawberries
Swiss chard
watercress

Summer

apricots
artichokes
beans
beets
bell peppers
blackberries
blueberries
broccoli
cabbage
cardoons
cauliflower
celery
cherries
chives
cilantro
corn
cucumbers
currants
dried beans
eggplant
English peas
fava beans
fennel
hot peppers
kale

lavender
lemongrass
melons
mint
mushrooms
okra
parsley
peaches
peas
plums
raspberries
romanesco
rosemary
sage
shallots
shell beans
snap peas
sprouts
string beans
summer squash
Swiss chard
tomatoes
turnips
watercress
zucchini

Fall

apples
black walnuts
broccoli
Brussels sprouts
cabbage
celeriac
dried beans
garlic
grains
grapes
green tomatoes
ground cherries
kale
leeks
lemongrass
mizuna
mushrooms
pears

peas
pecans
potatoes
pumpkins
radishes
raspberries
romanesco
sage
salsify
shallots
shell beans
sprouts
sweet potatoes
Swiss chard
tomatillos
turnips
winter squash

Winter

apples
beets
black radishes
black walnuts
bok choy
broccoli
Brussels sprouts
carrots
celeriac
chestnuts
dried beans
garlic
horseradish
kale
lemongrass

mizuna
mushrooms
onions
parsnips
pecans
potatoes
rutabaga
salsify
shallots
spinach
sprouts
sweet potatoes
Swiss chard
turnips
winter squash

Contributors

The following farmers, customers, chefs, vendors, and volunteers contributed recipes to this book.

Erika Allen, farmer,
Growing Power, Inc.

Hannah Altshuler, customer

Malika Ameen, chef/owner,
ByMDesserts

Rick Bayless, co-owner/chef,
Frontera Grill, Topolobampo,
XOCO; Green City Market
founding member

Dana Benigno, former
executive director,
Green City Market

Dominic Benigno, customer

Jennifer Berman, customer

Benjamin Browning, chef/
instructor, Kendall College,
School of Culinary Arts

George Bumbaris, co-owner/
chef, Prairie Grass Café

Tim Burton, farmer, Burton's
Maplewood Farm

Linda Calafiore, Green City
Market founding member

Marilyn Canna, volunteer

Phillippa Cannon, volunteer

Christine Cikowski, co-owner/
chef, Sunday Dinner Club,
Honey Butter Fried Chicken

Dave Cleverdon, farmer,
Kinnikinnick Farm; Green City
Market board member

Maria Concannon, owner,
Don Juan's Ristorante

Elizabeth Crawford, customer

Ted Dobbels, customer

Chris Djuric, customer;
assistant to the Mandel family

Beth Eccles, farmer, Green
Acres Farm; Green City Market
board member

Joel Espe, farmer,
Hawks Hill Elk Ranch

Betsy Fimoff, customer

Jacqueline Fisch, customer

Gale Gand, chef/founding
partner, Tru

Virginia Gerst, Green City
Market board member

Lynn Gerstein, customer

Robin Goldberg, customer

Melissa Graham, volunteer

Rita Gutekanst, principal,
Limelight Catering; Green City
Market board member

Carol Mighton Haddix,
customer

Jason Hammel, co-owner/
chef, Lula Café; co-owner,
Nightwood Restaurant

Judith Dunbar Hines, customer

Sandra Holl, vendor,
Floriole Café and Bakery

Meme Hopmayer, volunteer

Tammy Hsu, customer

Stephanie Izard, executive
chef, Girl & the Goat, Little
Goat Diner

Peter Klein, farmer,
Seedling Farms

Chris Koetke, vice president,
Kendall College, School of
Culinary Arts

Michael Kornick, owner/chef,
MK, DMK Burger Bar, Fish Bar,
Ada Street, County Barbeque

Corrine Kozlak, customer

Joshua Kulp, co-owner/chef,
Sunday Dinner Club, Honey
Butter Fried Chicken

Cindy Kurman, Green City
Market board member

Laura Lamar, customer

Pam Lamaster-Millett, customer

Adrienne Lawrence, customer

Amelia Levin, volunteer

Karen Levin, volunteer

Dana Cox Lipe, vendor,
The Honest Meal Project

Janine MacLachlan, volunteer

Mary McMahon, chef,
Elawa Farm

Tamera Mark, farmer,
Iron Creek Farm

Audrey Miller, customer

Carrie Nahabedian, owner/
chef, Brindille, Naha; Green
City Market board member

Megan Neubeck,
executive chef, Terzo Piano

Sharon Olson, customer

Kathy Paddor, Green City
Market board member

Alison Parker, farmer,
Radical Root Organic Farm

Michael Paulsen, owner/chef,
Abigail's American Bistro

Nancy Potter, vendor, Potter's
Organic Artisan Crackers

Joan Reardon, customer

Jill Remenar, customer

Elizabeth Richter, Green City
Market board member

Lou Ann Robinson, farmer,
Jake's Country Meats

Harriet Rosenman, customer

Noe Sanchez, executive chef,
Convito Café and Market

Abby Klug Schilling, farmer,
Mick Klug Farm

Diane Schmidt, customer

Sheri Schneider, customer

Jeanne Sexton, farmer,
Meadow Haven Farm

Debbie Sharpe, owner, Feast
Restaurant, The Goddess and
Grocer

Bruce Sherman, owner/chef,
North Pond; Green City Market
board member

Nancy Silver, vendor,
Snookelfritz Ice Cream Artistry

Alderman Michele Smith,
customer

Carol Smoler, volunteer

Pat Sondgeroth, farmer,
Heartland Meats

Peter Stasiulis, customer

Sarah Stegner, co-owner/chef,
Prairie Grass Café; Green City
Market founding member and
board co-chair

Laura Sterkel, volunteer

Judith Stockdale, customer

Karen Theis, customer

Rick Turley, customer

Marsha Goldsmith Van,
volunteer

Jill Van Cleave, customer

Jason Vincent, chef,
Nightwood Restaurant

Paul Virant, owner/chef,
Perennial Virant, Vie Restaurant

Jessica Volpe, vendor,
Pasta Puttana

Tracey Vowell, farmer, Three
Sisters Garden; Green City
Market board member

Jenny Yang, vendor,
Phoenix Bean

Shelley Young, CEO/founder,
The Chopping Block

Randy Zweiban, chef,
SRZ Consulting

Acknowledgments

We owe our thanks to all of those who submitted recipes and told the stories included in this book. As we paged through the submissions, we were consistently impressed by the creative use of the local, sustainably raised produce available at the Market, and were inspired by the accounts of what made each recipe special to the cook who offered it to us.

Many talented people donated their services to make this book a reality.

Despite a busy schedule that would leave lesser mortals reeling, Rick Bayless generously agreed to write the book's foreword, and literary agent Amy Collins of Squid Ink offered her expertise for love, not money.

Our publisher, Doug Seibold, and editor, Kate DeVivo, were wellsprings of ideas and models of patience, while Green City Market board co-chairs Sarah Stegner and John Berghoff added their strong support whenever we called for it. Erin Riley-Strong, the Market's communications coordinator, cheerfully added to her already-busy workload to help at all stages of the book's development.

The handsome photographs are the work of Chris Cassidy and creative photo stylist Nancy Cassidy, who were tireless in their determination to get the best shots. Jayson Home & Garden generously provided many of the artisan tabletop items and furnishings used in the photos.

Webitects, which provides ongoing support for the Green City Market website, programmed a special page to help market this book, and the Fleishman-Hillard team mapped an innovative plan for our social and media relations to help promote the book regionally and nationally.

Finally, we give thanks to the farmers and vendors who bring the best of the Midwest bounty to the Market, and to the shoppers, volunteers, and chefs who turn out to support them. Green City Market is more than a shopping venue. It is a family united in a passion for locally grown, sustainably raised food. We appreciate each and every person who contributes to this very happy place.

Index